OPPOSING
VIEWPOINTS®
SERIES

US Airport Security

Other Books of Related Interest:

Opposing Viewpoints Series

The Arab Spring

Civil Liberties

Racial Profiling

At Issue Series

Does the World Hate the United States?

Mexico's Drug Wars

Should the United States Close Its Borders?

Current Controversies Series

Espionage and Intelligence

Human Trafficking

Islamophobia

"Congress shall make no law ... abridging the freedom of speech, or of the press."

First Amendment to the US Constitution

The basic foundation of our democracy is the First Amendment guarantee of freedom of expression. The Opposing Viewpoints series is dedicated to the concept of this basic freedom and the idea that it is more important to practice it than to enshrine it.

OPPOSING
VIEWPOINTS®
SERIES

| US Airport Security

Margaret Haerens and Lynn M. Zott, Book Editors

GREENHAVEN PRESS
A part of Gale, Cengage Learning

GALE
CENGAGE Learning·

Detroit • New York • San Francisco • New Haven, Conn • Waterville, Maine • London

5|13   #809412026

Elizabeth Des Chenes, *Director, Publishing Solutions*

© 2013 Greenhaven Press, a part of Gale, Cengage Learning.

Gale and Greenhaven Press are registered trademarks used herein under license.

For more information, contact:
Greenhaven Press
27500 Drake Rd.
Farmington Hills, MI 48331-3535
Or you can visit our Internet site at gale.cengage.com

For product information and technology assistance, contact us at

Gale Customer Support, 1-800-877-4253
For permission to use material from this text or product, submit all requests online at www.cengage.com/permissions

Further permissions questions can be emailed to permissionrequest@cengage.com

Articles in Greenhaven Press anthologies are often edited for length to meet page requirements. In addition, original titles of these works are changed to clearly present the main thesis and to explicitly indicate the author's opinion. Every effort is made to ensure that Greenhaven Press accurately reflects the original intent of the authors. Every effort has been made to trace the owners of copyrighted material.

Cover Image copyright © ssuaphotos/Shutterstock.com.

LIBRARY OF CONGRESS CATALOGING-IN-PUBLICATION DATA

US airport security / Margaret Haerens and Lynn M. Zott, book editors.
    p. cm. -- (Opposing viewpoints)
    Includes bibliographical references and index.
    ISBN 978-0-7377-6040-8 (hardcover) -- ISBN 978-0-7377-6041-5 (pbk.)
    1. Airports--Security measures--United States--Juvenile literature. I. Haerens, Margaret. II. Zott, Lynn M. (Lynn Marie), 1969-
    HE9797.4.S4U82 2013
    363.28'76--dc23
                                                  2012041368

Printed in the United States of America
1 2 3 4 5 6 7 17 16 15 14 13

Contents

Chapter 3: Should Profiling Be Used as a Security Strategy?

Chapter 4: What Ongoing Issues Affect Airport Security?

Why Consider
Opposing Viewpoints?

> *"The only way in which a human being can make some approach to knowing the whole of a subject is by hearing what can be said about it by persons of every variety of opinion and studying all modes in which it can be looked at by every character of mind. No wise man ever acquired his wisdom in any mode but this."*
>
> John Stuart Mill

In our media-intensive culture it is not difficult to find differing opinions. Thousands of newspapers and magazines and dozens of radio and television talk shows resound with differing points of view. The difficulty lies in deciding which opinion to agree with and which "experts" seem the most credible. The more inundated we become with differing opinions and claims, the more essential it is to hone critical reading and thinking skills to evaluate these ideas. Opposing Viewpoints books address this problem directly by presenting stimulating debates that can be used to enhance and teach these skills. The varied opinions contained in each book examine many different aspects of a single issue. While examining these conveniently edited opposing views, readers can develop critical thinking skills such as the ability to compare and contrast authors' credibility, facts, argumentation styles, use of persuasive techniques, and other stylistic tools. In short, the Opposing Viewpoints Series is an ideal way to attain the higher-level thinking and reading skills so essential in a culture of diverse and contradictory opinions.

In addition to providing a tool for critical thinking, Opposing Viewpoints books challenge readers to question their own strongly held opinions and assumptions. Most people form their opinions on the basis of upbringing, peer pressure, and personal, cultural, or professional bias. By reading carefully balanced opposing views, readers must directly confront new ideas as well as the opinions of those with whom they disagree. This is not to argue simplistically that everyone who reads opposing views will—or should—change his or her opinion. Instead, the series enhances readers' understanding of their own views by encouraging confrontation with opposing ideas. Careful examination of others' views can lead to the readers' understanding of the logical inconsistencies in their own opinions, perspective on why they hold an opinion, and the consideration of the possibility that their opinion requires further evaluation.

Evaluating Other Opinions

To ensure that this type of examination occurs, Opposing Viewpoints books present all types of opinions. Prominent spokespeople on different sides of each issue as well as well-known professionals from many disciplines challenge the reader. An additional goal of the series is to provide a forum for other, less known, or even unpopular viewpoints. The opinion of an ordinary person who has had to make the decision to cut off life support from a terminally ill relative, for example, may be just as valuable and provide just as much insight as a medical ethicist's professional opinion. The editors have two additional purposes in including these less known views. One, the editors encourage readers to respect others' opinions—even when not enhanced by professional credibility. It is only by reading or listening to and objectively evaluating others' ideas that one can determine whether they are worthy of consideration. Two, the inclusion of such viewpoints encourages the important critical thinking skill of objectively evaluating an author's credentials and bias. This evaluation will illuminate an author's reasons for taking a particular stance on an issue and will aid in readers' evaluation of the author's ideas.

It is our hope that these books will give readers a deeper understanding of the issues debated and an appreciation of the complexity of even seemingly simple issues when good and honest people disagree. This awareness is particularly important in a democratic society such as ours in which people enter into public debate to determine the common good. Those with whom one disagrees should not be regarded as enemies but rather as people whose views deserve careful examination and may shed light on one's own.

Thomas Jefferson once said that "difference of opinion leads to inquiry, and inquiry to truth." Jefferson, a broadly educated man, argued that "if a nation expects to be ignorant and free . . . it expects what never was and never will be." As individuals and as a nation, it is imperative that we consider the opinions of others and examine them with skill and discernment. The Opposing Viewpoints series is intended to help readers achieve this goal.

David L. Bender and Bruno Leone,
Founders

Introduction

> *"We've achieved much since 9/11 in terms of collecting information that relates to terrorists and potential terrorist attacks, but it's becoming clear that the system that has been in place for years now is not sufficiently up to date to take full advantage of the information we collect and the knowledge we have."*
>
> —Barack Obama,
> speech, December 29, 2009

On November 24, 1971, a man using the name Dan Cooper (subsequently known as D.B. Cooper) boarded a Northwest Orient flight from Portland to Seattle. Once the plane was safely in the air, he passed a note to the flight attendant informing her that he had a bomb and would detonate it unless he was given $200,000. After landing in Seattle, releasing the rest of the passengers, and receiving the ransom money, Cooper forced the plane to take off again with only a skeleton flight crew to fly him to Mexico. While in flight, however, Cooper opened the aft door and parachuted out of the plane. He was never found.

The success of the D.B. Cooper skyjacking inspired a series of similar attempts of air piracy around the United States during the 1970s. By that time, there had already been political hijackings in other countries, and sky marshals were introduced on American flights in response to the increasing numbers of hijackings occurring all over the world. The innocent days of air travel—characterized by a lack of airport security—were over.

The Federal Aviation Agency (FAA), known today as the Federal Aviation Administration, began to meet the emerging and existing threats to the airline industry with new regulations, procedures, and security strategies developed to protect crews, passengers, and airports from hijacking and terrorist violence. In late 1972, the FAA put in place a regulation that all airlines had to begin screening passengers and their carry-on baggage by having them go through metal detectors. This screening was performed by private security companies, who were hired by the airline that held operational control over certain airline terminals based on a competitive bidding process.

On December 21, 1988, terrorists blew up Pan Am Flight 103 over Lockerbie, Scotland, killing 270 people. In response to the tragedy, the FAA implemented a number of new security measures to address terrorist threats: it began to advise airlines on security risks and intelligence information; it put in place more rigorous screening procedures for computers, radios, and other electronic equipment; and it required that only bags accompanied by a passenger be allowed on the plane.

The terrorist attacks on the United States on September 11, 2001—referred to as 9/11—generated renewed interest in airport security and reformed the US government's entire security strategy and infrastructure. On September 11, 2001, nineteen hijackers took control of four commercial airliners and aimed the planes at targets in the United States. The first plane, American Airlines Flight 11, which took off that morning from Logan International Airport in Boston, hit the North Tower of the World Trade Center in New York City. United Airlines Flight 175, which also originated at Logan, slammed into the South Tower. The third airliner crashed into the Pentagon in Arlington, Virginia, just outside Washington, DC. The fourth airliner crashed into a field in rural Shanksville, Pennsylvania, after passengers realized what was happening and tried to take back control of the plane from the hijackers.

The fact that terrorists could successfully smuggle weapons onto an American commercial airliner and then hijack four planes while in the air was deeply shocking. US legislators quickly moved to review all existing security procedures, propose reforms, and implement improved measures to protect the industry and US national security. Two months after 9/11, Congress enacted the Aviation and Transportation Security Act (ATSA), which federalized airport security and created the Transportation Security Administration (TSA) to oversee it. The TSA hired and trained passenger and baggage screeners to replace the private companies that had done the job prior to 9/11. The act also mandated that all checked bags be screened for explosives.

Airport security strategies focused on keeping dangerous objects off airplanes; that meant screening for knives, guns, and other things that could be used as weapons. New weapons led to changes in security procedures. When a British man, Richard Reid, unsuccessfully attempted to set off some plastic explosives he had hidden in his shoe on an international flight on December 21, 2001, the TSA quickly mandated that all shoes must be removed and put through the carry-on baggage screener during the passenger screening process. After intelligence surfaced that terrorists might try to hide explosives in liquid containers in order to blow up an American-bound plane, the TSA banned liquids from planes in 2006. In October 2010, after terrorists attempted to blow up cargo planes by filling toner cartridges with plastic explosives, the TSA banned toner and ink cartridges weighing over sixteen ounces.

On Christmas Day 2009, a young Nigerian man named Umar Farouk Abdulmutallab boarded a flight in Amsterdam to Detroit, Michigan, and right before the plane was scheduled to land, ignited plastic explosives that he had sewn into his underwear. Fortunately, the device failed, and four passengers jumped in to forcibly subdue Abdulmutallab until he could be arrested in Detroit. A year later, the TSA introduced new procedures, including full-body scanners and invasive pat downs. Many security experts believe that these new search procedures would have caught the explosive device hidden on Abdulmutallab and will discourage potential terrorists from trying similar measures.

However, as the TSA implemented these new security measures, there was growing criticism from the American public. Many scoffed at dumping liquids at checkpoints or taking off their shoes to be screened, claiming it was nothing more than "security theater" that did nothing to make passengers safer. Others took offense at the new full-body scans and invasive pat downs, deeming the new procedures to be ineffective, insensitive, and a violation of civil liberties. The American Civil Liberties Union (ACLU) called the full-body scans a "virtual strip search." Another focal point of criticism was the TSA philosophy of treating every passenger as a potential threat, sometimes leading to young children being searched or people in wheelchairs being interrogated by TSA agents.

In August 2011, the TSA began testing a risk-based approach to airport security. Instead of treating every passenger the same, a risk-based strategy mandates that TSA screeners assess the risk of each passenger by utilizing behavior detection techniques to determine whether a passenger is lying or hiding information. It also means developing programs to expedite the screening process for experienced travelers, children, and military, as well as focusing on more likely threats.

The TSA also emphasizes its "layers of security" approach to airport security. As stated on the TSA website: "We use layers of security to ensure the security of the traveling public and the nation's transportation system. Because of their visibility to the public, we are most associated with the airport checkpoints that our Transportation Security Officers operate. These checkpoints, however, constitute only one security layer of the many in place to protect aviation. Others include intelligence gathering and analysis, checking passenger manifests against watch lists, random canine team searches at airports, federal air marshals, federal flight deck officers and more security measures both visible and invisible to the public."

The authors of the viewpoints in *Opposing Viewpoints: Airport Security* assess the role of the TSA and the efficacy of some of the new security strategies implemented to protect the US commercial airline industry in chapters titled Does Airport Security Work?, Are Passenger Screening Policies Effective?, Should Profiling Be Used as a Security Strategy?, and What Ongoing Issues Affect Airport Security? The discussion in this volume provides information on the focus of airport security policies and the tension between implementing rigorous airport security and protecting the civil liberties of passengers.

OPPOSING
VIEWPOINTS®
SERIES

CHAPTER 1

Does Airport Security Work?

Chapter Preface

On December 25, 2009, a Northwest Airlines flight en route to Detroit, Michigan, from Amsterdam was the target of a failed terrorist attack when a passenger attempted to set off plastic explosives hidden in his underwear. Umar Farouk Abdulmutallab, a twenty-three-year-old Nigerian man associated with the terrorist group al Qaeda, had become inspired by the militant cleric Anwar al-Awlaki to take part in a terrorist plot to blow up an American-bound airplane. On Christmas Day 2009, Abdulmutallab boarded the flight to Detroit and only minutes before it was to land, ignited the explosive device sewn into his underwear. The device failed, but it set off a fireball that engulfed Abdulmutallab's pants and the wall and carpeting of the plane. Four passengers jumped in to forcibly subdue Abdulmutallab until he could be arrested in Detroit.

The incident shook the confidence of many Americans who believed and hoped that airport security had improved since the terrorist attacks of September 11, 2001. In that horrific series of attacks, nineteen al Qaeda terrorists hijacked four American airliners and used them as weapons to destroy American landmarks and kill innocent people. Eight years later, another al Qaeda terrorist, Abdulmutallab, had attempted an attack against American passengers and crew. The Christmas Day bombing attempt ignited a simmering debate on the efficacy of airport screening and its success in preventing a catastrophic terrorist attack.

In an attempt to cast light on the issue, the secretary of the Department of Homeland Security, Janet Napolitano, threw gasoline on the fire during an interview on CNN when she stated that "what we are focused on is making sure that the air environment remains safe, that people are confident when they travel. And one thing I'd like to point out is that the system worked. Everybody played an important role here. The passengers and crew of the flight took appropriate action. Within literally an hour to 90 minutes of the incident occurring, all 128 flights in the air had been notified to take some special measures in light of what had occurred on the Northwest Airlines flight. We instituted new measures on the ground and at screening areas, both here in the United States and in Europe, where this flight originated. So the whole process of making sure that we respond properly, correctly and effectively went very smoothly."

A day later, Napolitano reversed course, admitting that the system failed miserably when it allowed Abdulmutallab to board the plane with plastic explosives in his underwear. A later report by the Senate Select Committee on Intelligence outlined fourteen systematic errors that led to the Christmas Day bombing attempt; these ranged from the failure to place Abdulmutallab on any terrorist watch list despite intelligence information that identified him as a potential threat to the inability of the Federal Bureau of Investigation (FBI) and the Central Intelligence Agency (CIA) to access important intelligence information on him when it mattered most. The Senate report underscored the key role that intelligence plays in preventing terrorist attacks against the commercial airline industry in the United States. The Christmas Day bombing attempt also intensified security concerns about the level of airport screening at foreign airports for flights to the United States.

On February 16, 2012, Abdulmutallab was sentenced to four consecutive life sentences plus fifty years for his role in the Christmas Day bombing attempt. Just a few months later, in May 2012, the CIA reported that it had thwarted a similar terrorist plot: an al Qaeda terrorist in Yemen had attempted to smuggle a more sophisticated, harder-to-detect bomb onto a flight bound for the United States. This time, the aspiring suicide bomber was stopped before he even reached the airport because of successful intelligence gathering and cooperation between the CIA and its foreign partners.

For many, the Christmas Day 2009 bombing attempt revealed the flaws in US airport security and underscored the need to consider different approaches to predicting and preventing terrorist attacks on the nation's airline industry. For others, the May 2012 incident reinforced the need to stay one step ahead of terrorists taking advantage of cutting-edge technology and equipment to attack the United States. The viewpoints in the following chapter examine the effectiveness of US airport security, focusing on the need for better airport perimeter security, a more rational foreign policy, and the most effective procedures when it comes to airport screening.

| *"The continuing expenditure on security may actually have made the United States less safe."*

Airport Security Measures Are Ineffective and Overpriced

Charles C. Mann

Charles C. Mann is a journalist and author. In the following viewpoint, he consults with security expert Bruce Schneier, who has asserted that most of the airport measures enacted since the terrorist attacks on the United States on September 11, 2001, referred to as 9/11, accomplish nothing in the way of security and are not worth the enormous cost. Mann refers to airport security as "security theater," designed to make it look like the government is taking steps to protect people but is really doing nothing. According to Schneier, the only useful measures since 9/11 are the reinforcement of cockpit doors; positive baggage matching; and teaching passengers to fight back against hijackers.

As you read, consider the following questions:

1. How many hijackers were involved in the 9/11 hijackings, according to the viewpoint?

2. According to Mann, how much has the United States spent on homeland security since 9/11?

3. As of 2008, how many names of potential terrorists does the author say were listed on a terrorist watch list compiled by the US government?

Not until I walked with Bruce Schneier toward the mass of people unloading their laptops did it occur to me that it might not be possible for us to hang around unnoticed near Reagan National Airport's security line. Much as upscale restaurants hang mug shots of local food writers in their kitchens, I realized, the Transportation Security Administration [TSA] might post photographs of Schneier, a 48-year-old cryptographer and security technologist who is probably its most relentless critic. In addition to writing books and articles, Schneier has a popular blog; a recent search for "TSA" in its archives elicited about 2,000 results, the vast majority of which refer to some aspect of the agency that he finds to be ineffective, invasive, incompetent, inexcusably costly, or all four.

As we came by the checkpoint line, Schneier described one of these aspects: the ease with which people can pass through airport security with fake boarding passes. First, scan an old boarding pass, he said—more loudly than necessary, it seemed to me. Alter it with Photoshop, then print the result with a laser printer. In his hand was an example, complete with the little squiggle the TSA agent had drawn on it to indicate that it had been checked. "Feeling safer?" he asked.

The Reaction to 9/11

Ten years ago, 19 men armed with utility knives hijacked four airplanes and within a few hours killed nearly 3,000 people. At a stroke, Americans were thrust into a menacing new world. "They are coming after us," CIA [Central Intelligence Agency] director George Tenet said of al-Qaeda. "They intend to strike this homeland again, and we better get about the business of putting the right structure in place as fast as we can."

The United States tried to do just that. Federal and state governments embarked on a nationwide safety upgrade. Checkpoints proliferated in airports, train stations, and office buildings. A digital panopticon of radiation scanners, chemical sensors, and closed-circuit television cameras audited the movements of shipping containers, airborne chemicals, and ordinary Americans. None of this was or will be cheap. Since 9/11 [referring to the terrorist attacks on the United States on September 11, 2001], the U.S. has spent more than $1.1 trillion on homeland security.

To a large number of security analysts, this expenditure makes no sense. The vast cost is not worth the infinitesimal benefit. Not only has the actual threat from terror been exaggerated, they say, but the great bulk of the post–9/11 measures to contain it are little more than what Schneier mocks as "security theater": actions that accomplish nothing but are designed to make the government look like it is on the job. In fact, the continuing expenditure on security may actually have made the United States less safe.

An Unpopular Viewpoint

The first time I met Schneier, a few months after 9/11, he wanted to bet me a very expensive dinner that the United States would not be hit by a major terrorist attack in the next 10 years. We were in Washington, D.C., visiting one of the offices of Counterpane Internet Security, the company he had co-founded in 1999. (BT, the former British Telecom, bought Counterpane seven years later; officially, Schneier is now BT's chief security technology officer.) The bet seemed foolhardy to me. Defense Secretary Donald Rumsfeld had just told the *Washington Times* that al-Qaeda was dispersing its killers all over the world.

From an airplane-hijacking point of view, Schneier said, al-Qaeda had used up its luck. Passengers on the first three 9/11 flights didn't resist their captors, because in the past the typical consequence of a plane seizure had been "a week in Havana." When the people on the fourth hijacked plane learned by cell phone that the previous flights had been turned into airborne bombs, they attacked their attackers. The hijackers were forced to crash Flight 93 into a field. "No big plane will ever be taken that way again, because the passengers will fight back," Schneier said. . . . The instigators of the two most serious post–9/11 incidents involving airplanes—the "shoe bomber" in 2001 and the "underwear bomber" in 2009, both of whom managed to get onto an airplane with explosives—were subdued by angry passengers.

Schneier's sanguine views had little resonance at a time when the fall of the twin towers was being replayed nightly on the news. Two months after 9/11, the [George W.] Bush administration created the Transportation Security [Administration], ordering it to hire and train enough security officers to staff the nation's 450 airports within a year. Six months after that, the government vastly expanded the federal sky marshal program, sending thousands of armed lawmen to ride planes undercover. Meanwhile, the TSA steadily ratcheted up the existing baggage-screening program, banning cigarette lighters from carry-on bags, then all liquids (even, briefly, breast milk from some nursing mothers). Signs were put up in airports warning passengers about specifically prohibited items: snow globes, printer cartridges. A color-coded alert system was devised; the nation was placed on "orange alert" for five consecutive years. Washington assembled a list of potential terror targets that soon swelled to 80,000 places, including local libraries and miniature-golf courses. Accompanying the target list was a watch list of potential suspects that had grown to 1.1 million names by 2008, the most recent date for which figures are available. Last year [2010], the Department of Home-

An Ineffective TSA

After 9/11 [the September 11, 2001, terrorist attacks on the United States], the consensus among lawmakers was that the U.S. would spend whatever was necessary to defend homeland security. Now, the TSA [Transportation Security Administration] is fighting for funding, promising to perform its job smarter and to close security loopholes. At the same time, the agency defends controversial huge expenditures, such as on body scanners, that have prompted a flood of complaints about invasion of privacy and possible health risks.

Jon Hilkevitch,
"Aviation Security Hassles, Weaknesses Persist,"
Chicago Tribune, *September 6, 2011.*

land Security, which absorbed the TSA in 2003, began deploying full-body scanners, which peer through clothing to produce nearly nude images of air passengers.

"Security Theater"

Bruce Schneier's exasperation is informed by his job-related need to spend a lot of time in Airportland. He has 10 million frequent-flier miles and takes about 170 flights a year; his average speed, he has calculated, is 32 miles an hour. "The only useful airport security measures since 9/11," he says, "were locking and reinforcing the cockpit doors, so terrorists can't break in, positive baggage matching"—ensuring that people can't put luggage on planes, and then not board them—"and teaching the passengers to fight back. The rest is security theater."

Remember the fake boarding pass that was in Schneier's hand? Actually, it was mine. I had flown to meet Schneier at

Reagan National Airport because I wanted to view the security there through his eyes. He landed on a Delta flight in the next terminal over. To reach him, I would have to pass through security. The day before, I had downloaded an image of a boarding pass from the Delta website, copied and pasted the letters with Photoshop, and printed the results with a laser printer. I am not a photo-doctoring expert, so the work took me nearly an hour. The TSA agent waved me through without a word. A few minutes later, Schneier deplaned, compact and lithe, in a purple shirt and with a floppy cap drooping over a graying ponytail.

Identifying the True Threats

The boarding-pass problem is hardly the only problem with the checkpoints. Taking off your shoes is next to useless. "It's like saying, Last time the terrorists wore red shirts, so now we're going to ban red shirts," Schneier says. If the TSA focuses on shoes, terrorists will put their explosives elsewhere. "Focusing on specific threats like shoe bombs or snow-globe bombs simply induces the bad guys to do something else. You end up spending a lot on the screening and you haven't reduced the total threat."

As I waited at security with my fake boarding pass, a TSA agent had darted out and swabbed my hands with a damp, chemically impregnated cloth: a test for explosives. Schneier said, "Apparently the idea is that al-Qaeda has never heard of latex gloves and wiping down with alcohol." The uselessness of the swab, in his view, exemplifies why Americans should dismiss the TSA's frequent claim that it relies on "multiple levels" of security. For the extra levels of protection to be useful, each would have to test some factor that is independent of the others. But anyone with the intelligence and savvy to use a laser printer to forge a boarding pass can also pick up a stash of latex gloves to wear while making a bomb. From the standpoint of security, Schneier said, examining boarding passes and swabbing hands are tantamount to performing the same test twice because the person you miss with one test is the same person you'll miss with the other.

After a public outcry, TSA officers began waving through medical supplies that happen to be liquid, including bottles of saline solution. "You fill one of them up with liquid explosive," Schneier said, "then get a shrink-wrap gun and seal it. The TSA doesn't open shrink-wrapped packages." I asked Schneier if he thought terrorists would in fact try this approach. Not really, he said. Quite likely, they wouldn't go through the checkpoint at all. The security bottlenecks are regularly bypassed by large numbers of people—airport workers, concession stand employees, airline personnel, and TSA agents themselves (though in 2008 the TSA launched an employee-screening pilot study at seven airports). "Almost all of those jobs are crappy, low-paid jobs," Schneier says. "They have high turnover. If you're a serious plotter, don't you think you could get one of those jobs?"

> *"When we stop to give thanks for all our blessings . . . , let's give thanks for the people who spend their days and nights working to stop the terrorists from succeeding—including the men and women of the [Transportation Security Administration]."*

Airport Security Is Critically Important and Vastly Underrated

Marc A. Thiessen

Marc A. Thiessen is an author, political columnist, and former White House speechwriter. In the following viewpoint, he proposes that Americans should express their appreciation to Transportation Security Administration (TSA) workers, who have been pummeled by unfair criticism and public indignities in recent years. Thiessen points out that in the months right after the September 11, 2001, terrorist attacks on the United States, when concerns over airport security were paramount, no American would complain about invasive body searches or rigorous screening procedures if it meant protecting airline passengers from ter-

rorism. He reminds readers that terrorist organizations like al Qaeda would love to attack again and that strategies like profiling and enhanced screening techniques are essential in the effort to fight terrorism.

As you read, consider the following questions:

1. According to a 2010 *Washington Post*–ABC News poll cited in the viewpoint, what percentage of Americans say that "the risk of terrorism on airplanes is not that great"?

2. How many passengers go through airport security in the United States each day during the holiday weekend, according to Thiessen?

3. What does Thiessen say was the name of the terrorist cell recruited to fly airplanes into the Library Tower in Los Angeles?

In the coming days [in 2010], millions of Americans will travel to celebrate the Thanksgiving holiday with family and friends. May I pose a novel idea? As we go through the airport screening line, let's stop and say "thanks" to the men and women of the TSA [Transportation Security Administration] who give up time with their families during the holidays to keep us safe from terror.

In the past few weeks, these patriots have been compared with Big Brother and accused of sexual assault. They've suffered the same kinds of public indignities the Left has heaped on the men and women of the CIA [Central Intelligence Agency]—being accused of engaging un-American and unlawful behavior for doing the difficult and unpleasant work of protecting the country. They deserve better.

A Shocking Debate

Can any of us imagine the debate we've had in recent weeks unfolding in the days immediately following Sept. 11, 2001 [also referred to as 9/11, when terrorists attacked the United States]? Would any of us have objected to the deployment of millimeter wave scanners had the technology been available then? The current uproar could happen only in a country that has begun to forget the horror of 9/11. Indeed, it appears many in the country have forgotten. A new *Washington Post–ABC News* poll found that 66 percent of Americans say that "the risk of terrorism on airplanes is not that great." *Sixty-six percent.*

This just four years after al-Qaeda nearly succeeded in blowing up seven transatlantic flights departing London's Heathrow Airport—with more than 1,500 passengers on board—headed for New York, Washington, Chicago, Montreal, Toronto, and San Francisco. This just eleven months after an al-Qaeda operative succeeded in sneaking a bomb onto a plane in his underwear and nearly blew it up over the city of Detroit. This just weeks after al-Qaeda succeeded in getting two package bombs on board aircraft—including passenger planes—that were designed to blow up over the eastern seaboard of the United States. If we have learned anything about al-Qaeda in the years since 9/11, it is that they are obsessively focused on destroying planes.

If a passenger who is supposed to be seated near us on our next flight has a bomb in his underwear, I suspect most of us would prefer that the explosive be uncovered when he tries to get through airport security—not when a Dutch tourist sees the passenger in the row ahead of him try to set it off and dives across the plane to stop him, as happened on a flight to Detroit last Christmas [in 2009].

Personal Experience

In the last two weeks, I have been through TSA screening eight times—and not once was I asked to go through the millimeter wave machine, or undergo an enhanced pat down. Odds are that most of the 2.2 million passengers who will go through airport security each day during this holiday weekend will have a similar experience. On the last leg of my trip, I finally asked to go through both procedures to see what all the fuss was about. No one touched my junk.

Some critics have argued that the terrorists are more likely to attack us in other ways that can't be stopped by the new screening procedures. That is the same argument the Left uses against ballistic missile defense. They say our enemies are more likely to attack us with suitcase nukes that have no fingerprints than with a ballistic missile that has a return address. Well, just because we face the danger of suitcase bombs does not mean that we should not defend against the danger of ballistic missile attacks. If a burglar wants to break into our homes, we all know he can bust through the window—but that does not mean we leave our front doors unlocked when we go to bed at night.

Airport Screening

The same logic applies to airport screening. Yes, the terrorists can try to sneak explosives on board in other ways (such as hiding them in body cavities). But if we stop screening for the methods they have attempted to use in the past—shoe bombs, liquid explosives hidden in sports drinks, and, yes, underwear bombs—we would be inviting them to use those methods again. Remember the outrage we all felt last Christmas that a terrorist managed to get through airport security with a bomb in his underwear? Well, imagine the outrage we would feel if it happened again because the TSA failed to deploy readily available technology that had a high likelihood of uncovering such a bomb—especially if the terrorist succeeded in blowing up the plane this time.

Some say it is ridiculous to apply screening procedures to children and the elderly. But we know that the terrorists have strapped bombs onto children and used them to get past our security in places like Iraq. Think they would hesitate to do

The Transportation Security Administration (TSA)

Both in the field and at headquarters, the TSA workforce is vigilant in ensuring the security of people and commerce that flow through our nation's vast transportation networks. TSA employs risk-based, intelligence-driven operations to prevent terrorist attacks and to reduce the vulnerability of the nation's transportation system to terrorism. Our goal at all times is to maximize transportation security to stay ahead of evolving terrorist threats while protecting privacy and facilitating the flow of legitimate travel and commerce. TSA's security measures create a multilayered system of transportation security that mitigates risk. We continue to evolve our security approach by examining the procedures and technologies we use, how specific security procedures are carried out, and how screening is conducted.

The TSA workforce occupies the front line in executing the agency's transportation security responsibilities in support of the nation's counterterrorism efforts. These responsibilities include security screening of passengers and baggage at 450 airports in the United States that facilitate air travel for 1.8 million people per day; vetting more than 14 million passengers and over 13 million transportation workers against the terrorist watch list each week; and conducting security regulation compliance inspections and enforcement activities at airports, for domestic and foreign air carriers, and for air cargo screening operations throughout the United States and at last point of departure locations internationally.

Statement of Chris McLaughlin, David Nicholson, Sean Byrne, and James Duncan, Before the Subcommittee on Transportation Security, US House of Representatives, March 28, 2012.

the same here in America? If we announce that children and older travelers are exempt from screening, the terrorists will use children and older travelers to get bombs onto planes.

Some argue that the enhanced screening is a violation of our Fourth Amendment rights. No, it is not. Unlike buying health insurance, buying a plane ticket is still a purely voluntary activity in this country. We all agree to submit to screening when we decide to travel by plane. If we don't want to go through the electronic screening, we can choose to have a pat down instead. And if we prefer neither, we can drive, take a bus, or travel train. No American is forced through the enhanced screening procedures against his or her will.

Profiling

Some say we should use profiling instead. Profiling should absolutely be a key part of our layered defenses against terrorist attack. But profiling alone is insufficient, and is not as easy as it may seem. Just as the terrorists adapt their tactics to get around our screening procedures, they will adapt to get around profiling. We know this because Khalid Sheikh Mohammed [KSM, a member of al-Qaeda] told us so. As I recount in my book, *Courting Disaster*, after KSM was captured and questioned by the CIA [Central Intelligence Agency], he told the agency that after the 9/11 attacks he assumed we would be profiling for Arab men—so he recruited a cell of Southeast Asian terrorists to carry out the "second wave" of attacks. This cell—known as the [Al] Ghuraba cell—included trained pilots and suicide operatives who had met with Osama bin Laden and pledged to carry out martyrdom missions for him. They were captured hiding out in Karachi, Pakistan, awaiting instructions from the al-Qaeda leadership. Their mission was to fly an airplane into the Library Tower in Los Angeles.

When al-Qaeda deployed an operative to blow up a plane over Detroit, they did not send an Arab man—they sent a Nigerian. The terror group al-Shabaab—al-Qaeda's new affiliate in East Africa—has recruited more than 20 American citizens as foreign fighters. Most are of Somali descent. One—Zachary Adam Chesser—is a white kid from Oakton, Va., who converted to Islam and is now serving a prison sentence for trying to join al-Shabaab as a foreign fighter. Al-Qaeda recruits suicide bombers from all over the world—including right here in the U.S. It is not a simple matter to profile against such a diverse array of threats. Profiling is essential, but it is not a replacement for effective airport security.

Appreciating the TSA

We need to be crystal clear: As we gather with our families to carve the Thanksgiving turkey, the terrorists are gathering as well—in caves in Waziristan, Yemen, East Africa, and other fronts in the war on terror—to plan the next attack. The tenth anniversary of the 9/11 attacks is less than a year away. Al-Qaeda planned to mark the fifth anniversary by blowing up seven planes headed to North America (which is why liquids in carry-on luggage are now required to be in containers no bigger than 3.4 ounces). They may very well be planning something equally spectacular for the tenth anniversary. So when we stop to give thanks for all our blessings this weekend, let's give thanks for the people who spend their days and nights working to stop the terrorists from succeeding—including the men and women of the TSA.

If you travel by plane this holiday weekend, you'll have a chance to do so in person.

> *"Although a certain anxious fixation would have been excusable in the immediate aftermath of the 2001 attacks, here it is a decade later and we're still pawing through people's bags in a hunt for what are effectively harmless items."*

Airport Security Strategies Have the Wrong Focus

Patrick Smith

Patrick Smith is an airline pilot and writer. In the following viewpoint, he contends that Transportation Security Administration (TSA) passenger screening policies are potentially self-destructive because they draw attention away from the true threats to airport security such as adequate scrutiny for explosives. Smith argues that the American mania for airport security has become self-defeating and that the TSA should move beyond its preoccupation with "pointy objects." He maintains that once the element of surprise was gone on September 11, 2001, the chances of any terrorist group, including al Qaeda, trying an inflight takeover scheme went down dramatically.

Patrick Smith, "Ten Years After 9/11, Airport Security Still Not Getting It," Salon.com, April 19, 2011. This article first appeared in Salon.com, at http://www.salon.com. An online version remains in the Salon archives. Reprinted by permission.

As you read, consider the following questions:

1. What does Smith say that Bangkok airport security confiscated from him?

2. What are the TSA's new "freeze drills," according to Smith?

3. Why does Smith say that the Massachusetts Port Authority is fighting the construction of a proposed nature trail along the northern perimeter of Logan International Airport?

At the Bangkok airport they took my scissors. This was the second time they took my scissors in Bangkok. I should have learned my lesson.

They were safety scissors, the kind you'd give to a child, about two-and-a-half inches long with rounded tips. Highly dangerous—at least as the BKK [Bangkok airport] security staff saw it. My airline pilot credentials meant nothing to them.

It's funny, but not really, when you stop to consider how easy it would be to fashion a sharp object—certainly one deadlier than a pair of rounded-end scissors—*after* boarding an airplane, from almost anything within your reach: a wine bottle, a first-class juice glass, a piece of plastic molding, and so on and so forth. Heck, if you're seated in first or business class, they *give you* a metal knife and fork.

But more to the point, pun intended, why do we still *care* so much about pointy objects?

The Wrong Mind-Set

When it came right down to it, the success of the Sept. 11 [2001] attacks had nothing—nothing—to do with box cutters. The hijackers could have used anything. They were not exploiting a weakness in luggage screening, but rather a weakness in our mind-set—our understanding and expectations of what a hijacking was and how it would unfold. The hijackers weren't relying on weapons, they were relying on the element of surprise.

All of that is different now. For several reasons, from passenger awareness to armored cockpit doors, the in-flight takeover scheme has long been off the table as a viable MO [modus operandi, or method of operation] for an attack. It was off the table before the first of the twin towers had crumbled to the ground. Why don't we see this? Although a certain anxious fixation would have been excusable in the immediate aftermath of the 2001 attacks, here it is a *decade* later and we're still pawing through people's bags in a hunt for what are effectively harmless items.

There in Bangkok it hit me, in a moment of gloomy clarity: These rules are never going to change, are they?

How depressing is that, to be stuck with this nonsense permanently? Not only the obsession with sharps, but the liquids and gels confiscations, the shoe removals, etc.

Self-Destructive Policies

These policies aren't just annoying, they're potentially self-destructive. Self-destructive because they draw our security resources away from more useful pursuits. Imagine if, instead of a tiny pair of scissors, I'd had a half pound of explosives in my luggage, shaped into some innocuous-looking item. Would the Bangkok screeners have caught it, or are they too busy hunting for pointy things and contraband shampoo? And what of passengers' checked luggage? Are the bags down below undergoing adequate scrutiny for explosives—a far more potent threat than somebody's hobby knife?

Making a bad situation worse, airline fees for checked luggage have resulted in unprecedented numbers of carry-on bags being dragged through concourse checkpoints. All bags undergo mandatory screening, it's true, be they carry-ons or checked bags. But what's changed is where and how these in-

"This Doesn't Look Like You," cartoon by Mike Flanagan, www.CartoonStock.com.

spections are taking place. Unfortunately, more carry-ons means greater emphasis on pawing through people's roll-aboards looking for benign implements. Frankly there should be a call to scale back the screening of carry-ons, or at least revise the kind of screening they currently undergo. Guards should not spend two seconds worrying about a pilot's—or anybody else's—safety scissors.

And what ever happened to that IATA [International Air Transport Association] proposal to develop a multi-tiered screening strategy that divides passengers into different risk groups, some receiving a higher level of scrutiny than others?

And have you heard, meanwhile, about the Transportation Security Administration's [TSA's] new "freeze drills"?

Freeze Drills

The *New York Times*'s "On the Road" columnist Joe Sharkey recently published a story describing an encounter with this odd and somewhat troubling procedure. Ostensibly it's a practice maneuver that helps TSA guards learn how to deal with checkpoint breaches. Guards begin yelling, "Code Bravo, freeze!" effectively scaring passengers into remaining motionless.

Of course, as Sharkey deftly points out, TSA doesn't really have the authority to make *anybody* remain motionless. TSA guards do not have law enforcement power—much as the agency has done a good job at fooling people into believing otherwise. Screeners are now called "officers" and they wear blue shirts with badges. Not by accident, the badges look exactly like the kind worn by police.

Thus the cynics out there see the freeze drills as a means of control and intimidation. They probably feel the same way about the recent revelation that "arrogant complaining about airport security" is an indicator used by screeners when looking for criminals and terrorists.

The Role of TSA

In both cases that's probably unfair, though TSA is, at times, prone to bullying and guilty of a certain mission creep. At the airport, TSA's job is to keep dangerous items and dangerous people away from planes, end of story. We can argue over the definition of dangerous, but TSA holds the authority—legitimately enough in my opinion—to inspect your belongings and prevent you from passing through a checkpoint. However, it does *not* have the authority to interrogate you, make you stand in one place, recite the national anthem or otherwise compromise your rights.

Joe Sharkey describes being upbraided not by a TSA guard, but by another passenger when he opted not to remain perfectly still during a freeze drill. Honestly, it's not the drills themselves that concern me so much as the idea of a fellow citizen so willing to concede his freedom. Welcome to America, 2011.

Just how rampant and self-defeating is our security mania? Let's step outside the terminal for a moment, into the fresh air. Here in Boston, the Massachusetts Port Authority [Massport] is fighting a proposed nature trail that would run along the northern perimeter of Logan International Airport. Massport fears the greenway would come too close to a bus depot it is building in the same area.

"They don't want the greenway anywhere near the proposed bus depot," wrote the *Boston Globe*'s Lawrence Harmon in an op-ed piece on April 10, "for fear that terrorists could penetrate the area and sabotage buses."

You read that correctly. Enough said. I'll just end it right there, and let that quote drift off into the air.

> "Our security ought to stop anything these days, stringent as it is: We've gone from the metal detectors of the 1970s to post–9/11 body scans and enhanced pat downs."

Airport Security Has Improved Since 9/11

Rick Seaney

Rick Seaney is the proprietor of FareCompare.com and a frequent commentator on the airline industry. In the following viewpoint, he maintains that airline travel is safer than it was when terrorists attacked the United States on September 11, 2001, also referred to as 9/11, due to enhanced security measures and the proactive attitude of passengers who have proved quick to react and subdue any possible threats in recent years. Seaney also notes the increased number of Transportation Security Administration (TSA) employees trained to spot possible threats in airports around the country. Although the level of security has gone up, Seaney believes that the system is far from perfect and the experience of flying has deteriorated across the board.

As you read, consider the following questions:

1. According to Seaney, what were the two reasons that bad guys hijacked planes in the United States before 9/11?

2. How many TSA employees does Seaney say there are in the United States?

3. What airline carriers does Seaney cite as having gone out of business since 9/11?

Do you remember how much courage it took to get on a plane in the weeks and months following 9/11 [referring to the terrorist attacks on the United States on September 11, 2001]? One of the first things a United pilot did when he returned to flying that September was to thank his passengers for their bravery; he also urged them to "stand up, together" against terrorists. The entire cabin erupted in applause.

Now it is ten years later and those fears are fading. If anything tells us that, it's the airfare prices for flights on the anniversary and so far, I am seeing no discounts for flying this Sept. 11, as there might be if the airlines expected a dip in ridership. On most major routes (at least as of a few days ago), you'll pay the same base airfare whether you fly Sept. 4 or Sept. 11 or Sept. 18.

I suspect this year [2011] some will see flying on 9/11 as something of a badge of honor. As it should be. Which brings me to perhaps the biggest change since the September terrorist attacks: the attitude of the flying public. We will never again be passive passengers.

Air Travel After 9/11: Is It Safer?

Passivity used to pay off; before 9/11, bad guys in the U.S. took over planes for one of two reasons, usually: to get somewhere (often Cuba) or to get something (such as D.B. Cooper's demand for $200,000). In most of those cases, passengers were released unharmed, so it stands to reason that many aboard the 9/11 planes figured they too would eventually be freed which gave the terrorists the element of surprise. I mean, who would have thought planes would be used as weapons?

We wised up quickly; in fact, the element of surprise disappeared altogether by the time the fourth plane was in the air over Pennsylvania. That's when a heroic band of passengers on United Flight 93 prevented their hijackers from using the plane against any final target.

Passengers have proved themselves again and again since 9/11, starting just a few months later: Several of them helped subdue Richard Reid, the so-called shoe bomber on an American Airlines flight that December; then, on Christmas Day 2009, a Northwest passenger thwarted the man known as the underwear bomber.

Has Flight Safety Improved Since 9/11?

So are we safer in the air since 9/11? Yes, thanks to passengers like these, and also thanks to a numbing array of new security measures. But security comes at a price and it comes with no guarantees. Our security ought to stop anything these days, stringent as it is: We've gone from the metal detectors of the 1970s to post–9/11 body scans and enhanced pat downs. Cockpit doors are now fortified, and the sky marshal program put into place by Pres. [Richard] Nixon has been expanded. Some pilots are even armed. But the biggest change has to be the sheer numbers of people watching out for us: the approximately 50,000 TSA [Transportation Security Administration] employees we see at the airports every time we fly.

At first, most accepted the TSA's water-bottle ban, the shoe removal, the possibility of an up-close-and-personal pat down; it's what we had to do to be safe. But as the years went by and the occasional gun or other dangerous item got through security even as stories about little kids and old ladies being singled

The Creation of the TSA and Regulations Following 9/11

We [the Transportation Security Administration (TSA)] were created in the wake of the terrorist attacks of September 11, 2001 [referred to as 9/11], to strengthen the security of the nation's transportation systems. The Aviation and Transportation Security Act, passed by the 107th Congress on November 19, 2001, established our agency and gave it three major mandates:

- responsibility for security for all modes of transportation;

- recruit, assess, hire, train, and deploy security officers for 450 commercial airports from Guam to Alaska in 12 months; and,

- provide 100 percent screening of all checked luggage for explosives by December 31, 2002.

In the largest civilian undertaking in the history of the U.S. government, we met these congressional deadlines. In March 2003, we were moved from the Department of Transportation to the Department of Homeland Security that was created on November 25, 2002, by the Homeland Security Act of 2002, unifying the nation's response to threats to the homeland.

Transportation Security Administration,
"How We Began," TSA.gov, 2012.

out for "special" treatment multiplied, critics became increasingly aggressive, sneering at security as "theater". Is it worth it? I'm sure it has thwarted some criminals, but the system is far from perfect.

The Flying Experience

In the meantime, the overall air travel experience since 9/11 has gone to hell in a handbasket.

Once planes began flying again, there were lots of empty seats—the fear factor again—which led the airlines to begin cutting capacity. That helped some carriers survive, but the sluggish economy was of no help, which led to the introduction of shocking new fees (American Airlines slapped on its first checked-bag fee in 2008). Still, a number of carriers went into bankruptcy anyway, while some like ATA [American Trans Air], Aloha, Skybus and more simply vanished.

Surviving airlines, meanwhile, kept cutting perks; food service, which was severely curtailed after 9/11, reached its zenith last fall when Continental offered the last free meal in coach. Speaking of customer service, if you want to talk to a human being at an airline, be prepared to fork over $25 for the privilege, but you may find the non-human airport kiosk quicker and more responsive.

What We Have Lost

What else have we lost since 9/11? A certain innocence, and something else; I suppose you could call it the joy of travel. Look around next time you're at the airport and see how people dress. Sweats, ratty jeans, and even saggy pants, but you know what? It's not inappropriate attire, not when you consider that flying these days is no longer a pleasant adventure, but a chore. The hassle of security, the difficult encounters with overworked airline employees; what is the point of dressing up like *Mad Men* extras for that?

But still we fly. We are wiser and way more cynical since 9/11, and we put up with more garbage than ever before, but we know no one is going to stop us from flying. The terrorists tried but ten years later, we keep getting on planes. We fly.

> "We now live not just with all the usual
> fears that life has to offer, but in some-
> thing like a United States of Fear."

True Airport Security Requires Rational and Effective US Foreign Policy

Tom Engelhardt

Tom Engelhardt is an author and editor of TomDispatch.com. In the following viewpoint, he suggests that America's aggressive and wrongheaded foreign policy has resulted in the invasive airport screening strategies that many people oppose. Engelhardt questions why Americans have been so passive about what the US government does in their name and yet only get outraged when that very same policy results in vigorous pat downs at the airport. He urges Americans to connect the dots between US foreign policy and the security state at home and realize that the terrorists are accomplishing one of their key goals: bankrupting America.

As you read, consider the following questions:

1. According to Engelhardt, what is the annual budget for the US intelligence bureaucracy?

2. About what two outrages does Engelhardt believe the American people have been remarkably quiet?

3. What is Operation Hemorrhage, according to the author?

It's finally coming into focus, and it's not even a difficult equation to grasp. It goes like this: Take a country in the grips of an expanding national security state and sooner or later your "safety" will mean your humiliation, your degradation. And by the way, it will mean the degradation of your country, too.

Just ask Rolando Negrin, a Transportation Security Administration (TSA) screener who passed through one of those new "whole body image" scanners last May [in 2010] as part of his training for airport security. His coworkers claimed to have gotten a look at his "junk" and mocked him mercilessly, evidently repeatedly asking, "What size are you?" and referring to him as "little angry man." In the end, calling it "psychological torture," he insisted that he snapped, which in his case meant that he went after a coworker, baton first, demanding an apology.

Consider that a little parable about just how low this country has sunk, how psychologically insecure we've become while supposedly guarding ourselves against global danger. There is no question that, at the height of Cold War hysteria, when superpower nuclear arsenals were out of this world and the planet seemed a hair trigger from destruction, big and small penises were in play, symbolically speaking. Only now, however, facing a ragtag set of fanatics and terrorists—not a mighty nation but a puny crew—are those penises perfectly real and, potentially, completely humiliating.

Failed Bombs Do the Job

We live, it seems, in a national security "homeland" of little angry bureaucrats who couldn't be happier to define what "safety" means for you and big self-satisfied officials who can duck the application of those safety methods. Your government can now come up with any wacky solution to American "security" and you'll pay the price. One guy brings a failed shoe bomb on an airplane, and you're suddenly in your socks. Word has it that bombs can be mixed from liquids in airplane bathrooms, and there go your bottled drinks. A youthful idiot flies toward Detroit with an ill-constructed bomb in his underwear, and suddenly they're taking naked scans of you or threatening to grope your junk.

Two bombs don't go off in the cargo holds of two planes and all of a sudden sending things around the world threatens to become more problematic and expensive. Each time, the price of "safety" rises and some set of lucky corporations, along with the lobbyists and politicians that support them, get a windfall. In each case, the terror tactic (at least in the normal sense) failed; in each case, the already draconian standards for our security were ratcheted up, while yet more money was poured into new technology and human reinforcements, which may, in the end, cause more disruption than any successful terror attack.

Directly or indirectly, you pay for the screeners and scanners and a labyrinthine intelligence bureaucracy that officially wields an $80 billion budget, and all the lobbyists and shysters and pitchmen who accompany our burgeoning homeland-security complex. And by the way, no one's the slightest bit nice about it either, which isn't surprising since it's a national security state we're talking about, which means its mentality is punitive. It wants to lock you down, quietly and with full acquiescence if possible. Offer some trouble, though, or step out of line, and you'll be hit with a $10,000 fine or maybe put in cuffs. It's all for your safety, and fortunately they have a set of the most inept terror plots in history to prove their point.

By now, who *hasn't* written about the airport "porno scans," the crotch gropes and breast jobs, the "don't touch my junk" uproar, the growing lines, and the exceedingly modest protests on the Wednesday before Thanksgiving, not to speak of the indignity of it all?

Totally been there, completely done that; totally written about, fully read. Shouldn't we move on?

Taking Off the Gloves (and Then Everything Else)

And yet there are a few dots that still need to be connected. After all, since the beginning of George W. Bush's second term, Americans have been remarkably quiet when it comes to the national security disasters being perpetuated in their name. America's wars, its soaring Pentagon budgets, its billion-dollar military bases, its giant new citadels still called embassies but actually regional command centers, its ever-escalating CIA [Central Intelligence Agency] drone war along the Pakistani tribal borderlands, the ever-expanding surveillance at home, and the incessant "night raids" and home razzings thousands of miles away in Afghanistan, not to speak of Washington's stimulus-package spending in its war zones have caused no more than the mildest ripple of protest, much less genuine indignation, in this country in years.

American "safety" has, in every case, trumped outrage. Now, for the first time in years, the oppressiveness of a national security state bent on locking down American life has actually gotten to some Americans. No flags are yet flying over mass protests with "Don't Scan on Me" emblazoned on them. Still, the idea that air travel may now mean a choice between a spritz of radiation and a sorta naked snapshot or—thrilling option B—having some overworked, overaggressive TSA agent grope you has caused outrage, at least among a minority of Americans, amid administration confusion. (If you want evidence that Hillary Clinton is considering a run for president in 2012, check out what she had to say about her lack of eagerness to be patted down at the airport.)

Local authorities have threatened to bring sexual battery charges against TSA agents who step over the line in pat downs. Some legislators are denouncing the TSA's new security plans. Ron Paul [congressman from Texas] has introduced the American Traveler Dignity Act. And good for them all.

Connecting the Dots

But here's the thing: In our deluded state, Americans don't tend to connect what we're doing to others abroad and what we're doing to ourselves at home. We refuse to see that the trillion or more dollars that continue to go into the Pentagon, the U.S. intelligence community, and the national security state yearly, as well as the stalemated or losing wars Washington insists on fighting in distant lands, have anything to do with the near collapse of the American economy, job devastation at home, or any of the other disasters of our American age.

As a result, those porno scanners and enhanced pat downs are indignities without a cause—except, of course, for those terrorists who keep launching their bizarre plots to take down our planes. And yet whatever inconvenience, embarrassment, or humiliation you suffer in an airport shouldn't be thought of as something the terrorists have done to us. It's what the American national security state that we've quietly accepted demands of its subjects, based on the idea that no degree of danger from a terrorist attack, however infinitesimal, is acceptable. (When it comes to genuine safety, anything close to that principle is absent from other aspects of American life where—from eating to driving, to drinking, to working—genuine danger exists and genuine damage is regularly done.)

We now live not just with all the usual fears that life has to offer, but in something like a United States of Fear.

So think of it as an irony that, when George W. Bush and his cronies decided to sally forth and smite the Greater Middle East, they exulted that they were finally "taking the gloves off."

And so they were: aggressive war, torture, abuse, secret imprisonment, souped-up surveillance, slaughter, drone wars, there was no end to it. When those gloves came off, other people suffered first. But wasn't it predictable—since unsuccessful wars have a nasty habit of coming home—that, in the end, other things would come off, and sooner or later they would be on you: your hat, your shoes, your belt, your clothes, and of course, your job, your world?

And don't for a second think that it's going to end here. What happens when the first terrorist with a suppository bomb is found aboard one of our planes? After all, such weapons already exist. In the meantime, the imposition of more draconian safety and security methods is, of course, being considered for buses, trains, and boats. Can trucks, taxis, cars, and bikes be far behind? After all, once begun, there can, by definition, be no end to the search for perfect security.

You Wanna Be Safer? Really?

You must have a friend who's extremely critical of everyone else but utterly opaque when it comes to himself. Well, that's this country, too.

Here's a singular fact to absorb: We now know that a bunch of Yemeni al-Qaeda adherents have a far better hit on just who we are, psychologically speaking, and what makes us tick than we do. Imagine that. They have a more accurate profile of us than our leading intelligence profilers undoubtedly do of them.

Recently, they released an online magazine laying out just how much the two U.S.-bound cargo-bay bombs that caused panic cost them: a mere $4,200 and the efforts of "less than six brothers" over three months. They even gave their plot a name, Operation Hemorrhage (and what they imagined hemorrhaging, it seems, was not American blood, but treasure).

Now, they're laughing at us for claiming the operation failed because—thanks reportedly to a tip from Saudi intelligence—those bombs didn't go off. "This supposedly 'foiled plot,'" they wrote, "will without a doubt cost America and other Western countries billions of dollars in new security measures. That is what we call leverage."

They are, they claim, planning to use the "security phobia that is sweeping America" not to cause major casualties, but to blow a hole in the U.S. economy. "We knew that cargo planes are staffed by only a pilot and a co-pilot, so our objective was not to cause maximum casualties but to cause maximum losses to the American economy" via the multibillion-dollar U.S. freight industry.

This is a new definition of asymmetrical warfare. The terrorists never have to strike an actual target. It's not even incumbent upon them to build a bomb that works. Just about anything will do. To be successful, they just have to repeatedly send things in our direction, inciting the expectable Pavlovian [predictable] reaction from the U.S. national security state, causing it to further tighten its grip (grope?) at yet greater taxpayer expense.

In a sense, both the American national security state and al-Qaeda are building their strength and prestige as our lives grow more constrained and our treasure vanishes.

Enacting Policy to Make America Safer

So you wanna be safer? I mean, *actually* safer? Here's a simple formula for beginning to improve American safety and security at every level. End our trillion-dollar wars in Afghanistan and Iraq; set our military to defending our own borders (and no, projecting power abroad does not normally qualify as a defense of the United States); begin to shut down our global empire of bases; stop building grotesque embassy-citadels abroad (one even has a decorative moat, for god's sake!); end our overseas war stimulus packages and bring some of that money home. In short, stop going out of our way to tick off foreigners and then pouring our treasure into an American war machine intent on pursuing a generational global war against them.

Of course, the U.S. national security state has quite a different formula for engendering safety in America: fight the Afghan war until hell freezes over; keep the odd base or two in Iraq; dig into the Persian Gulf region; send U.S. special operations troops into any country where a terrorist might possibly lurk; and make sure the drones aren't far behind. In other words, reinforce our war state by ensuring that we're eternally in a state of war, and then scare the hell out of Americans by repeatedly insisting that we're in imminent danger, that shoe, underwear, and someday butt bombers will destroy our country, our lives, and our civilization. Insist that a single percent of risk is 1% too much when it comes to terror and American lives, and then demand that those who feel otherwise be dealt with punitively, if they won't shut up.

It's a formula for leaving you naked in airports, while increasing the oppressive power of the state. And here's the dirty, little, distinctly Orwellian secret: the national security state can't do without those Yemeni terrorists (and vice versa), as well as our homegrown variety. All of them profit from a world of war. You don't—and on that score, what happens in an airport line should be the least of your worries.

The national security state is eager to cop a feel. As long as Americans don't grasp the connections between our war state and our "safety," things will only get worse and, in the end, our world will genuinely be in danger.

"If today a person can still slip undetec-ted both onto the tarmac of a major airport and then slip into the landing gear compartment of a U.S. airliner undetected, aviation security definitely deserves a deeper and more serious re-view."

Airport Perimeter Security Must Be Strengthened

Daniel Kaufmann

Daniel Kaufmann is a senior fellow in the Global Economy and Development program at the Brookings Institution. In the fol-lowing viewpoint, he argues that the recent discovery of a dead stowaway in the landing gear compartment of a Delta plane shows that aviation safety is essential outside of the airport ter-minal. Kaufmann suggests that if a person can slip undetected onto the tarmac of a major US airport and then hide in the landing gear compartment of a plane, there is a fundamental flaw in airport security in the United States that must be ad-dressed as soon as possible. He proposes that a thorough security investigation take place and new policies be implemented to ad-dress the systemic security failure at the heart of the incident.

As you read, consider the following questions:

1. According to the viewpoint, at what airport in Japan did a maintenance worker find the dead body of a stowaway in the landing gear compartment of a Delta plane on February 7, 2010?

2. Why does Kaufmann believe that the dead stowaway was not a tarmac employee at JFK airport in New York City?

3. From where do some apologists contend the stowaway may have originated, according to the author?

In a previous critical opinion on the Transportation Security Administration's (TSA's) implementation of new profiling guidelines in response to the Christmas Day terrorist attempt [in which Umar Farouk Abdulmutallab tried to set off a bomb on Northwest Airlines Flight 253 on December 25, 2009], I pointed to the inconsistent governance criteria applied in compiling their watch list of countries and proposed a shift in focus away from nationality profiling. Instead, I suggested a multi-pronged strategy that might prove both more efficient and effective in detecting and deterring terrorist threats. The strategy would entail increased and earlier focus on the person (rather than mere belongings), emphasizing scrutiny of visa applications and review of passports, expert observation of behavior, and effective use of a well-integrated background database of high-risk individuals.

Considering Airport Perimeter Security

Recent events have also made clear the necessity of explicitly focusing on what I had left out as the obvious: Aviation safety is essential outside of the airport terminal as well. Closely guarding of entry and movements on the airport tarmac, and the comings and goings around idle aircraft is also fundamental. The freezing death of a stowaway during last weekend's [in February 2010] Delta flight from New York's JFK airport [John

F. Kennedy International Airport] to Tokyo's Narita [Narita International Airport] is a rude reminder that we cannot take the obvious for granted, and that aviation security remains flawed at a very basic level.

If today a person can still slip undetected both onto the tarmac of a major airport and then slip into the landing gear compartment of a U.S. airliner undetected, aviation security definitely deserves a deeper and more serious review—over and above that which has been suggested in the aftermath of the Christmas Day bombing attempt.

A Dead Stowaway

Last Sunday, February 7th, a maintenance worker at Narita airport in Japan found the body of a dead stowaway in the landing gear compartment of the Delta Boeing 777 aircraft. Intriguingly, even though four full days have since elapsed, details of the man's identity, point of origin, and possible security lapses have yet to emerge publicly. In addition, the media coverage was very modest at first and then disappeared altogether, in spite of the dire safety implications of this incident.

Even with little information at this stage, it is unlikely that the apparent stowaway was a tarmac employee at JFK since he would have known that his action would result in almost certain death. It thus appears that there was a double security breach—first entering and wandering into the tarmac itself and then slipping into the landing gear bay of the aircraft. Both breaches are troublesome. The landing gear, while unpressurized, is sizable and can hold an adult and/or lethal explosives.

Inside the airport terminal, TSA personnel screened every child and grandmother for even the tiniest tubes of toothpaste. Yet, an adult could have easily slip undetected onto the tarmac and aircraft with a bomb, which fortunately was not the case here.

Perimeter Security Is a Shared Responsibility

Unlike checkpoint security, which is carried out exclusively by TSOs [transportation security officers], perimeter security for airports' secured areas is a mutual responsibility shared among federal, state, and local government personnel. TSA [Transportation Security Administration] also depends upon law enforcement personnel and resources provided by the airport authority, state or local government or airport personnel to play a lead role in carrying out perimeter security responsibilities.

John Sammon,
Testimony Before the US House of Representatives,
Committee on Oversight and Reform, July 13, 2011.

A Dangerous Hole in Security

In attempts to lessen the relevance of this event, some may point out that every so many years a dead stowaway is found in some exposed bay of an airplane. However, in today's security theater, where terrorist innovation cannot be underestimated, such rationale is feeble and reckless. This is particularly so for U.S. airliners, which are serious potential targets for terrorists.

Other apologists may try to suggest that the same Delta aircraft may have traveled from other countries (possibly Africa) over the days prior to landing at JFK (before flying to Tokyo), and that the stowaway may have originated abroad (in an African airport instead, implying that the stowaway would have been dead in that compartment for many days).

But even then the case for an aviation security revamp in the U.S. would still be compelling. Under such circumstances, there would have been a monitoring and security failure prior to the flight's departure to New York's JFK airport, along with a failure at the JFK airport to detect a stowaway while the aircraft sat on the tarmac. In fact, a security inspection of any aircraft about to travel on an international route is supposed to take place a couple of hours before departure, which makes it more likely that the stowaway may have slipped into the aircraft hold at JFK.

Thus, ... much silence and mystery have surrounded the circumstances of this case. But in light of previous serious mishaps, a scrupulous investigation into this incident should take place, and the government investigative and regulatory agencies ought to be fully transparent with the public as to what actually took place. The investigation into this incident ought to be complemented by a review into a possible broader systemic security failure and the need for a broader aviation safety revamp than originally envisaged in the aftermath of the Christmas Day would-be-bomber mishap.

In sum, this latest stowaway incident, while tragic for only one man who did not seem to have any terrorist intention, does further the case for a revamp of the U.S. approach to aviation security. For starters, there is a need to "think outside of the terminal" as well as outside of the box regarding the conventional approach to TSA security within airport terminals. And in moving outside of the "terminal-only" mind frame, U.S. aviation security in collaboration with other countries ought to review tarmac security wherever U.S. airliners fly and revisit how airliners are monitored and secured.

Periodical and Internet Sources Bibliography

The following articles have been selected to supplement the diverse views presented in this chapter.

Harriet Baskas	"How the Airport Experience Has Changed Since 9/11," *USA Today*, September 7, 2011.
Dick Cavett	"Flying? Increasingly for the Birds," *Opinionator* (blog), *New York Times*, August 19, 2011.
Jonathan Cronin	"Ten Years Later: Post-9/11 Airport Security as Farce," Open Salon, September 10, 2011. http://open.salon.com.
Jessica Dickler	"Post 9/11 Travel: What Airport Security Costs Us," CNN Money, September 8, 2011. http://money.cnn.com.
Jon Hilkevitch	"Aviation Security Hassles, Weaknesses Persist," *Chicago Tribune*, September 6, 2011.
Scott Mayerowitz	"Do You Really Believe You Are Safe at the Airport?," ABC News, June 23, 2010.
Scott McCartney	"Aiming to Balance Security and Convenience," *Wall Street Journal*, September 1, 2011.
Robert Poole	"Will We Get Serious About Aviation Security?," *Reason*, December 29, 2009.
Bruce Schneier	"Clear Common Sense for Takeoff: How the TSA Can Make Airport Security Work for Passengers Again," *New York Daily News*, June 23, 2009.
John Stossel	"Has Our Security Since 9/11 Been Worth $8 Trillion?," FoxNews.com, September 7, 2011.
Alex Wagner	"Airport Security: Joke's on Us!," Politics Daily, January 4, 2010. www.politicsdaily.com.

CHAPTER 2

Are Passenger Screening Policies Effective?

Chapter Preface

In March 2012, a major controversy erupted when a video was posted to YouTube showing a twenty-seven-year-old American man, Jonathan Corbett, allegedly sneaking a metallic object through two different full-body scanners at two different airports. As Corbett stated in the video, he set out to prove that the new advanced imaging technology (AIT) scanners installed in more than 180 US airports were ineffective because they would not be able to detect metallic weapons positioned in certain ways on the body. To prove his theory, he sewed a pocket into his shirt, placed a metallic case in it, and then went through an AIT body scanner at the Ft. Lauderdale-Hollywood International Airport in Florida. According to Corbett, he passed through the security checkpoint without Transportation Security Administration (TSA) screeners detecting anything on him—even though he underwent a full-body scan for the express purpose of finding just such an object. Next, Corbett alleged that he did the same thing at Cleveland Hopkins International Airport: He placed the same metal carrying case in the secret pocket in his shirt and made it through the full-body scan easily.

As Corbett explained in the video, he launched his investigation into the efficacy of the TSA's full-body scanners because of his concern for US national security and his outrage over the waste of American tax dollars on failed TSA policies. "Now, I'm sure the TSA will accuse me of aiding the terrorists by releasing this video, but it's beyond belief that the terrorists haven't already figured this out and are already plotting to use this against us," he contends. "It's also beyond belief that the TSA did not already know everything I just told you, and arrogantly decided to disregard our safety: anything to force Americans to give up our liberty to the federal government and our tax dollars to companies that are in bed with that government. . . . So let's fix this problem—now—before the terrorists take this opportunity to hurt us. The TSA must immediately end the nude body scanner program, and return to the tried-and-true metal detectors that actually work, and work without invading our privacy, as well as implement better solutions for nonmetallic explosives, such as bomb-sniffing dogs and trace detection machines."

Within days, Corbett's YouTube video went viral and reignited the controversy over the full-body scanners, which had already drawn criticism from many Americans who felt that the machines violated their privacy by showing images of their naked or nearly naked bodies to TSA agents. However, for many people, the scanners would be bearable if they were effective and protected passengers and crews from hidden weapons that could be used in an attack in the air. Now, with alleged proof that AIT technology was fatally flawed and that weapons could easily pass through the screening process, it inspired a new wave of anti-AIT protests.

The TSA quickly responded to the video and the controversy. In a post on *The TSA Blog*, Bob Burns wrote, "For obvious security reasons, we can't discuss our technology's detection capability in detail; however, TSA conducts extensive testing of all screening technologies in the laboratory and at airports prior to rolling them out to the entire field. Imaging technology has been extremely effective in the field and has found things artfully concealed on passengers as large as a gun or nonmetallic weapons, on down to a tiny pill or tiny baggies of drugs. It's one of the best tools available to detect metallic and nonmetallic items, such as . . . you know . . . things that go BOOM."

Burns went on to explain that the full-body scanners are just part of an overall security strategy, "one layer of our 20 layers of security (behavior detection, explosives detection canines, federal air marshals, etc.) and is not a machine that has all the tools we need in one handy device. We've never claimed it's the end all be all."

The debate over the efficacy of the full-body scanners deployed at major airports around the United States is just one of the topics discussed in the following chapter, which focuses on the TSA's passenger screening policies. Other issues examined include the safety and value of AIT technology, whether the new scanners violate civil liberties, and the question of how passenger screening policies affect religious modesty.

"*Every day, we strive to ensure our operational planning and decision-making process is timely, efficient and as coordinated as possible—and critically, based on intelligence.*"

Passenger Screening Policies Are Effective, Safe, and Respectful of Privacy

John S. Pistole

John S. Pistole is the administrator of the Transportation Security Administration (TSA). In the following viewpoint, he outlines the progress and successes that the TSA has made in airline security in the years since the terrorist attacks on the United States on September 11, 2001. Pistole asserts that the TSA strives to address emerging threats and to protect passenger privacy with cutting-edge technological advancements. The TSA also is implementing a risk-based security strategy, which, Pistole explains, allows the TSA to identify and deal with threats to the US transportation network as well as offer expedited screening for passengers who qualify.

John S. Pistole, "Counterterrorism, Risk-Based Security and TSA's Vision for the Future of Aviation Security," TSA.gov, March 5, 2012.

As you read, consider the following questions:

1. How many "peace officers," now known as air marshals, were in the first class sworn in fifty years ago, according to the viewpoint?

2. According to Pistole, how many passengers has the TSA screened since 2002?

3. How many guns does Pistole say were detected at airport checkpoints in 2011?

Last fall [in 2011], we marked the 10th anniversary of both the September 11, 2001 [referred to as 9/11], terrorist attacks and the legislation known as ATSA—the Aviation and Transportation Security Act—passed by the United States Congress as an important part of our country's response to those horrific attacks.

The Transportation Security Administration [TSA] was created through that legislation, and we continue to be proud of how TSA was staffed and operational in less than one year. Many Americans don't know that building TSA required the largest, most complex mobilization of the federal workforce since World War II.

As TSA administrator, I work closely with many dedicated individuals who know our agency's story better than anyone because they helped write it.

Protecting Americans

At the top of that list is TSA deputy administrator Gale Rossides, one of just a handful of public servants given the urgent task of [setting] up a new security agency whose sweeping mission has always been to protect our nation's transportation systems to ensure the freedom of movement for people and commerce.

At its core, the concept of risk-based security demonstrates a progression of the work TSA has been doing throughout its first decade of service to the American people. It is an understanding, really an acknowledgment, that we are not in the business of eliminating all risk associated with traveling from point A to point B. Risk is inherent in virtually everything we do. Our objective is to mitigate risk and to reduce, as much as possible, the potential for anyone to commit a deliberate attack against our transportation systems.

Before I begin, I want to take just a moment to mention another significant anniversary within the TSA family. Last Friday, March 2nd [2012], the men and women of the Federal Air Marshal Service, who today comprise TSA's primary law enforcement component, celebrated their 50th anniversary.

Originally safety inspectors for the FAA [Federal Aviation Administration], the first class of 18 "peace officers" as they were called then, was sworn in 50 years ago and began building the legacy of protection which today's officers uphold every time they board an aircraft. While their core mission to protect the flying public has remained constant over the years, federal air marshals today have an ever-expanding role in homeland security and they work closely with other law enforcement agencies to accomplish their mission.

Air marshals today are integrated with our partners such as the National Counterterrorism Center, the National Targeting Center, and on the FBI's [Federal Bureau of Investigation's] Joint Terrorism Task Forces.

They are a critical part of the effective partnerships that are essential to nearly everything we do.

Before TSA

To help set the stage for the emergence of the risk-based, intelligence-driven transportation security system we are building at TSA, it helps to take a brief look back and recall that transportation security before the September 11th terrorist attacks bears little resemblance to the strong, multilayered system in place today. This is especially true with respect to aviation security.

Remember that before September 11, 2001, there was:

- No cohesive system in place to check passenger names against terrorist watch lists in advance of flying;

- Only limited technologies in place for uncovering a wide array of threats to passengers or aircraft;

- No comprehensive federal requirements to screen checked or carry-on baggage;

- Minimal in-flight security on most flights; and,

- From a coordination standpoint, before 9/11 there was a lack of timely intelligence sharing, in both directions—from the federal level down to the individual airports, as well as from an individual airport up to the national level.

I came to TSA more than a year and a half ago, having worked the previous 26 years in a variety of positions within the FBI. That experience, with a range of partners inside the law enforcement and intelligence communities, helped shape my approach to solidifying TSA's place within the national counterterrorism continuum.

What TSA Does

Every day, we strive to ensure our operational planning and decision-making process is timely, efficient and as coordinated as possible—and critically, based on intelligence. We work to share critical information with key industry stakeholders whenever appropriate, and we are constantly communicating with our frontline officers through shift briefings held several times a day.

Thanks to the effective partnerships we've forged with industry stakeholders, with our airline and airport partners, and with law enforcement colleagues at every level, TSA has achieved a number of significant milestones during its first 10 years of service.

These include matching 100 percent of all passengers flying into, out of, and within the United States against government watch lists through the Secure Flight program.

It includes screening all air cargo transported on passenger planes domestically and, as you know, we work closely with our international partners every day to screen 100% of high-risk inbound cargo on passenger planes. We're also working hard with these same partners to screen 100% of all international inbound cargo on passenger planes by the end of this year.

And it also includes improving aviation security through innovative technology that provides advanced baggage screening for explosives.

Since their inception in 2005 through February 2012, we have also conducted more than 26,000 visible intermodal prevention and response, or VIPR, operations. We have 25 multi-modal VIPR teams working in transportation sectors across the country to prevent or disrupt potential terrorist planning activities.

Additionally, since 2006, TSA has completed more than 190 baseline assessments for security enhancement for transit, which provides a comprehensive assessment of security programs in critical transit systems.

TSA Accomplishments

We are seeing the benefits of how these important steps—combined with our multiple layers of security, including cutting-edge technology—keep America safe every day.

Since our stand up in 2002, we have screened nearly six billion passengers. Our frontline officers have detected thousands of firearms and countless other prohibited items and we have prevented those weapons from entering the cabin of an aircraft.

In fact, more than 10 years after 9/11, TSA officers still detect, on average, between three and four firearms every day in carry-on bags at security checkpoints around the country.

Deploying advanced, state-of-the-art technologies continues to factor significantly into our multilayered approach to transportation security. In particular, we continue to see the efficacy of advanced imaging technology, or AIT, machines at hundreds of passenger security checkpoints around the United States.

From February 2011 to June 2011, the Office of Inspector General (OIG) assessed the manner in which TSA inspects, maintains and operates backscatter units used in passenger screening.

The OIG found that TSA was in compliance with standards regarding radiation exposure limits and safety requirements. As a result of intensive research, analysis, and testing, TSA concludes that potential health risks from screening with backscatter X-ray security systems are minuscule.

While there is still no perfect technology, AIT gives our officers the best opportunity to detect both metallic and non-metallic threats including improvised explosive devices such as the device Umar Farouk Abdulmutallab attempted to detonate on Christmas Day, 2009.

Adapting to New Threats

As manufacturers continue enhancing the detection capability and strengthening the privacy features of their machines, we maintain the ability to upgrade the software used on them to stay ahead of the rapidly shifting threat landscape. Maintaining a high level of adaptability enables us to keep an important technological advantage.

Throughout 2011, this and other technologies helped our officers detect hundreds of prohibited, dangerous, or illegal items on passengers.

These "good catches" as we call them, illustrate how effective our people, process and technology are at finding concealed metallic and nonmetallic items concealed on a passenger or in their bags.

In an ongoing effort to help educate the traveling public, we highlight many of these good catches every week in blog posts uploaded to TSA.gov. I hope some of you have seen these. They have included incidents of items concealed in shoes, to weapons hidden in a hollowed out book, to ceramic knives, to exotic snakes strapped to a passenger's leg. As strange as some of these tales may be, they are a stark reminder that now—more than 10 years after the September 11, 2001, attacks—people are still trying to bring deadly weapons onto aircraft. And our officers are detecting numerous weapons every day and keeping them off of planes.

Less than one month ago in fact, over Presidents' Day weekend in February, our officers detected 19 guns in carry-on bags at various checkpoints around the country. In total, 1,306 guns were detected at airport checkpoints in 2011.

Protecting Privacy of Passengers

It's important to note that, while working hard to deploy the latest technological advancements to secure transportation, we have also taken significant steps to strengthen privacy protections for passengers screened with advanced imaging technology.

Last fall, we upgraded all of our millimeter wave units nationwide with new privacy protection software called automated target recognition. This software upgrade further enhances privacy protections by eliminating passenger-specific images and displaying instead a generic outline of a person.

We know that this software also makes the process more efficient. Any time a piece of new technology strengthens security, provides enhanced privacy protections and gives greater resource efficiency—that's a winning formula for all travelers.

The TSA's New Prescreening Initiative

TSA [Transportation Security Administration] Pre✔™ is a prescreening initiative that allows passengers to volunteer information about themselves prior to traveling domestically to expedite their checkpoint screening at participating airports. The initiative is part of the agency's broader effort to implement risk-based concepts that enhance aviation security by focusing more on travelers the agency knows the least about and allowing known travelers the opportunity to expedite their travel through security checkpoints.

"The continued growth and passenger participation in the TSA Pre✔™ initiative affirms our commitment to the evolution of our intelligence-driven, risk-based approach," [TSA administrator John S.] Pistole said. "This initiative is a testament to the outstanding collaborative work between TSA, CBP [U.S. Customs and Border Protection], airports, airlines, and the traveling public." . . .

Eligible passengers include U.S. citizens of frequent-flyer programs on participating airlines and current members of CBP Trusted Traveler Programs, including Global Entry, SENTRI [Secure Electronic Network for Travelers Rapid Inspection] and NEXUS.

Transportation Security Administration,
"Risk-Based Security Initiative Reaches Key Milestone,"
TSA.gov, May 3, 2012.

As good as they are, technologies such as this one do not stand alone. That's why we continue our efforts to strengthen, whenever possible, standard operating procedures already in place throughout the roughly 450 airports we secure.

Risk-Based Security Strategy

One of the ways we're doing this is by developing and putting into practice a series of risk-based, intelligence-driven processes to further strengthen aviation security. In 2011, we implemented several new screening concepts, including a program designed to verify the identity of airline pilots, and provided expedited screening adjustments in screening procedures for children 12 and under and the use of expanded behavior detection techniques.

Perhaps the most widely known security enhancement we are putting in place is TSA Pre✓™, one of several risk-based, intelligence-driven measures currently helping our agency move away from a one-size-fits-all security model and closer to its goal of providing the most effective transportation security in the most efficient way possible. One-size-fits-all was necessary after 9/11 and has been effective, but thanks to two key enablers, technology and intelligence, we're able to move toward a risk-based security model.

These initiatives are enabling us to focus our resources on those passengers who could pose the greatest risk—including those on terrorist watch lists—while providing expedited screening, and perhaps a better travel experience, to those we consider our low-risk, trusted travelers.

The Success of TSA Pre✓™

We began implementing this idea last fall and since then, at the nine airports currently participating, more than 460,000 passengers around the country have experienced expedited security screening through TSA Pre✓™ and the feedback we've been getting is consistently positive.

The success of TSA Pre✓™ has been made possible by the great partnerships with our participating airlines and airports and our sister component, CBP [U.S. Customs and Border Protection].

The airlines work with us to invite eligible passengers to opt into the initiative and working with CBP we are able to extend TSA Pre✔™ benefits to any U.S. citizen who is a member of one of CBP's Trusted Traveler Programs, like Global Entry.

I encourage anyone who is interested to apply for Global Entry. If you get accepted, you get benefits from both CBP and TSA at participating airports.

By the end of 2012, we expect to be offering passengers in 35 of our busiest airports the expedited screening benefits associated with TSA Pre✔™.

The Goals of Risk-Based Security

By constantly evaluating new ideas and adding strength to layers of security throughout the screening process, we can accomplish several things.

First of all, these efforts allow our officers to focus their attention on those travelers we believe are more likely to pose a risk to our transportation network. Focusing our efforts in a more precise manner is not only good for strengthening aviation security, but also for improving the overall travel experience for the millions of people who fly in the United States every day.

Later this month TSA will begin evaluating additional risk-based, intelligence-driven changes to checkpoint security screening procedures.

Our ability to find the proverbial needle in the haystack is improved every time we are able to reduce the size of the haystack. Strengthening our screening procedures with risk-based initiatives such as TSA Pre✔™ is getting this done, and we will continue expanding this program whenever we can.

We also continue to explore ways to adjust our standard security screening procedures for certain segments of the general traveling public—as we did last year with younger travelers.

The Military

In addition to expanding our use of intelligence, we are also using the risk-assessment model that drives the airline industry's known crewmember effort in other ways. By the end of the month, we will expand the TSA Pre✔™ population to include active-duty U.S. Armed Forces members with a common access card, or CAC, traveling out of Reagan National Airport. Service members will undergo the standard TSA Secure Flight prescreening and if we are able to verify the service member is in good standing with the Department of Defense by scanning their CAC card at the airport, they will receive TSA Pre✔™ screening benefits, such as no longer removing their shoes or light jacket and allowing them to keep their laptop in its case and their 3-1-1 compliant bag in a carry-on.

In addition to active-duty members of the United States Army, Navy, Air Force, Marine Corps and Coast Guard, this evaluation will also include active drilling members of the U.S. National Guard and reservists.

U.S. service members are entrusted to protect and defend our nation and its citizens with their lives, and as such TSA is recognizing that these members pose little risk to aviation security.

Constant Reevaluation

As we review and evaluate the effectiveness of these possible enhancements, additional changes to the security screening process may be implemented in the future as TSA continues to work toward providing all travelers with the most effective security in the most efficient way possible.

Of course, TSA will always retain the ability to incorporate random and unpredictable security measures throughout the airport, and no individual is ever guaranteed expedited screening.

We appreciate the ongoing support and cooperation of the aviation industry and the traveling public as we strive to continue strengthening transportation security and improving, whenever possible, the overall travel experience for all Americans. There are also significant economic benefits to strengthening aviation security, most notably in the area of cargo security and our ability to facilitate the secure movement of goods. The interconnectedness and interdependence of the global economy requires that every link in the global supply chain be as strong as possible. Whether it is for business or for pleasure, the freedom to travel from place to place is fundamental to our way of life, and to do so securely is a goal to which everyone at TSA is fully committed.

> *"Even the most modest of us would probably agree to a brief flash of quasi-nudity if it would really ensure a safe flight. That's not the deal the [Transportation Security Administration] is offering."*

Passenger Screening Policies Violate Privacy and Do Not Ensure Security

Noah Shachtman

Noah Shachtman is a contributing editor at Wired *magazine and a nonresident fellow at the Brookings Institution. In the following viewpoint, he maintains that the enhanced passenger screening policies implemented by the Transportation Security Administration (TSA) are ineffective and invasive. Shachtman points out that terrorists have already figured out ways to work around the full-body scanners, rendering them of limited value. However, he is encouraged by the TSA's adoption of a more risk-based system that focuses on true threats to airport security.*

As you read, consider the following questions:

1. What is "National Opt-Out Day," according to Shachtman?

2. How many scanners does Shachtman say there were in sixty-eight airports as of 2010?

3. How many more TSA employees does Shachtman say were needed to man the scanners?

In May [2010], Transportation Security Administration [TSA] screener Rolando Negrin pummeled a coworker with his government-issued baton. The feud began, according to a Miami-Dade Police Department report, after Mr. Negrin's training session with one of the agency's whole-body imagers. The scan "revealed [Mr. Negrin] had a small penis," the disgruntled coworker told police. After a few months, he "could not take the jokes anymore and lost his mind."

Now the TSA is rolling out these ultra-revealing imagers across the country in an attempt to uncover hidden threats like the so-called underwear bomb found on a Detroit-bound flight last Christmas [in 2009]. The agency and the scanners' manufacturers insist they've installed features and instituted procedures that will make passenger embarrassments impossible.

The Backlash Against Body Scanning

Privacy advocates aren't buying it. They've sued the Department of Homeland Security, asking a federal judge for an "emergency stay" of the body-scanning program. They're also calling on passengers to refuse the scans next week during a "National Opt-Out Day." Separately, unions representing American Airlines and US Airways pilots told their members to skip the screenings—on Opt-Out Day and every other.

But the larger question is whether the TSA's tech-centric approach to security makes any sense at all. Even the most modest of us would probably agree to a brief flash of quasi-nudity if it would really ensure a safe flight. That's not the deal the TSA is offering. Instead, the agency is asking for Rolando Negrin–style revelations in exchange for incremental, uncertain security improvements against particular kinds of concealed weapons.

Magical Thinking

It's the same kind of trade-off TSA implicitly provided when it ordered us to take off our sneakers (to stop shoe bombs) and to chuck our water bottles (to prevent liquid explosives). Security guru Bruce Schneier, a plaintiff in the scanner suit, calls this "magical thinking . . . descend on what the terrorists happened to do last time, and we'll all be safe. As if they won't think of something else." Which, of course, they invariably do. Attackers are already starting to smuggle weapons in body cavities, going where even the most adroit body scanners do not tread. No wonder that the Israelis, known for the world's most stringent airport security, have so far passed on the scanners.

Today, 373 are installed in 68 U.S. airports. One thousand machines are supposed to be in place by the end of next year. And the [President Barack] Obama administration has requested 5,355 additional employees to man the scanners—at a cost of $219 million in the first year alone. The only alternative to the screeners will be a pat down from a TSA worker.

The TSA uses two models of body scanner. One zaps the passenger with a tiny amount of X-rays that penetrate the clothes, but stop at the skin. The other scanner uses millimeter waves—a close cousin of microwaves—to pull off the same trick. (Regarding radiation exposure, the FDA [U.S. Food and Drug Administration] says there's "no more than a minimal risk to people being scanned.") By measuring the direction and frequency of the waves that come back, the system can tell what's beneath a traveler's garments.

A Privacy Problem?

TSA officials say that's not a privacy problem. Under new TSA guidelines, they point out, the person looking at the scanned image is in an entirely separate room, and the picture is deleted as soon as the next passenger steps into the scanner.

The images themselves are also altered for modesty—at least for the moment. TSA officials even claim that Mr. Negrin's privates weren't really exposed. Rapiscan Systems, which makes the backscatter X-ray scanner, installs one of a series of "privacy algorithms" that can dial up or down the images' resolution. (Of course, the fuzzier the result, the harder it is to spot a weapon.) Similarly, millimeter scanner–maker L-3 can blur faces, chests and groins, depending on the customer's preference. Individual employees, the companies promise, will not be able to alter these settings. However, top authorities at TSA will have the flexibility to make a policy change. They can keep the images comparatively blurry—or not.

A Risk-Based Approach

There may be an important policy shift in the works. TSA has long hewed to an unthinking, unbending approach to security that brought the agency a level of admiration ordinarily reserved for health insurers. But in his first five months running the agency, TSA chief John [S.] Pistole has sent some encouraging signs that he's absorbed the arguments of TSA's critics. "We can't just look for prohibited items on a list. We've got to provide the best security while giving greater scrutiny to those who need greater scrutiny, and not using a cookie-cutter approach for everybody," he says.

But Mr. Pistole holds to his view about body scanners' "important role in the future of aviation security," adding that the TSA is looking into new privacy enhancements. Unfortunately for Rolando—and the rest of us—the scanners appear to be here to stay.

> *"It's the world we inhabit, where threats are unpredictable, and non-state actors keep us terrorized, and guessing, and on our guard."*

Passenger Screening Policies Are Efficient and Worthwhile

Marcia DeSanctis

Marcia DeSanctis is a writer and journalist. In the following viewpoint, she argues that body scanners would be a "godsend" for people like her; she has titanium material in her body from an operation years ago. Usually, DeSanctis must undergo a rigorous pat down from Transportation Security Administration (TSA) personnel that she describes as a bit "ridiculous"—but worthwhile if it keeps her and other passengers safe. But with the use of body scanners, she anticipates passenger screening will be efficient, time saving, and not as invasive as other methods.

As you read, consider the following questions:

1. What did doctors do to DeSanctis's leg to relieve years of excruciating pain from a congenitally misshapen hip joint?

2. What did doctors give DeSanctis to explain the metal body parts that would set off airport security?

3. According to the author, what kind of comments have TSA employees made while giving her full-body pat downs?

Just in time for the holidays, new revelations about airport pat downs have suddenly sparked the nation's ire. As if traveling in the era of al-Qaeda isn't odious enough, now we're obliged to toss our downsized toiletries if they're not in a one-quart Ziploc. We're herded along the conveyor belt, forced into a disturbing intimacy with strangers, as we remove our shoes like a bunch of dutiful kindergarteners. But for anyone like me, who bears an extra load of surgically implanted metal, travel has long been a frustrating, often revolting endeavor. That's why I saw deliverance for the first time in full-body scanners. For me, they're a godsend.

A Major Procedure

My hip replacement was no big deal. I was relatively young for the procedure. Except for the hockey player whose trashed body needed an overhaul, most of my fellow post-ops inching down the corridors on walkers were older than me. But when they sliced off my leg and installed a foot-long titanium shaft with three wood screws, the years-long agony from the grinding and scraping of a congenitally misshapen hip joint, discovered when I was nineteen, was finally over.

After my third follow-up visit, when my scar had diminished to a tiny, puckered strip, the surgeon told me I could fly again. My hip felt so good I wasn't sure I even needed a plane. Nevertheless, the receptionist handed me a white plastic card. It bore my name and a fancy hospital logo; it was my preemptive explanation for the great din my new metal body part would inevitably incite at airport security. It looked about as authentic as my official Wyatt Earp's driver's license that I

The Benefits of Advanced Imaging Technology

- Improves security effectiveness by displaying metallic and nonmetallic anomalies.

- Enhances passenger experience by minimizing need for physical pat downs.

- Ensures privacy by placing the security officer viewing the image in a remote location, using privacy filters, and not having capability to store or transfer images.

- Improves security effectiveness by reducing physical fatigue of security personnel and improving their effectiveness through training and image detection technique.

- Is a highly effective security tool. In fact, the technology has led to the detection of more than 300 prohibited, illegal or dangerous items at checkpoints nationwide since January 2010.

"Advanced Imaging Technology Safety and Health Program,"
2011 Joint Meeting of American Association of Physicist
sin Medicine and Canadian Organization of Medical Physicists,
August 3, 2011.

picked up at a gift shop in Tombstone. Nevertheless, I was optimistic the first time I flew after the operation. Bursting with entitlement, I presented the card to the TSA [Transportation Security Administration] employee at the security checkpoint. "That's a joke, right?" the checker asked. Chastened, I walked through the machine. The buzzer beeped and then for the first time, I heard the official yell those two hated words: "Female assist."

A Female Assist

He screamed it, I would soon learn, because the one female on duty is frequently AWOL, or else engaged in another body search of a ninety-year-old woman with a pacemaker or two metal knees. Usually, he'll scream it again. And again. And again, and I stand there with the clock ticking, listening to the boarding announcements, hoping at this point to make my flight.

Recently at LAX [Los Angeles International Airport], I waited twenty minutes for a woman to emerge, and I regret to say that my equanimity failed me. Usually, I'm resigned and compliant, hating every minute of it. I understand that these folks don't make the rules. But this time, I went nuts on the guy, as he called and called—not loudly enough, I noted repeatedly—for a female assist. I told him I would sign a waiver indicating my willingness to be searched by a man. I offered to rip off my clothes. I begged to go look for a woman myself—after all, they were in possession of my phone, computer, wallet, money, suitcase and shoes. I would leave my watch, for good measure. Traveler after traveler passed me by, looking at me as if I were a prisoner in the stockades. I needed to get home, and the probability of making my flight was growing dim.

And here's what happens in these pat downs. First, she does a full scan with her wand, and when she finds metal, she tells me she's going to use the back of her hand to investigate it manually. Of course, all the metal is over the naughty bits. The underwire in the bra sets off the alarm, as do the grommets and zipper of my jeans. As does the offending hip joint, which starts behind my pelvic bone, on the right hindquarter. Even in form-fitting trousers, my behind gets the once over, about six or seven times. So, yes, she touches and feels and rubs and pats. And sometimes, makes conversation. I've been complimented on the color of my toenail polish. My weight has frequently been remarked on, as has my suntan, and even a mole on my abdomen. Many TSA employees want to chew the fat about my hip replacement, either as an added security measure or, I suspect, to mitigate their own sense of absurdity. I imagine they're asking themselves, Why does my job require that I flay this nice woman? Do I really think her bra is carrying a detonator?

The Reality of Today's World

And in spite of it all, none of this really bothers me. It's inconvenient, time consuming and frankly, ridiculous. But if the nation thinks these pat downs are going to keep us safer, then I support it. It's the world we inhabit, where threats are unpredictable, and non-state actors keep us terrorized, and guessing, and on our guard. I'll admit that I can't understand the logic of being able to travel with five different electronic devices and their chargers, but not my foundation makeup or my face cream. But if one day, someone tries to smuggle an explosive in her bra, the authorities will be prepared.

I don't actually believe my privacy is being violated, or that the women who pay too much attention to my groin have anything in mind besides doing the job that they're required to do. It's never occurred to me to complain to the TSA, even when my children watch me get pawed and prodded from the sidelines. The sense I get from the female assists is that they know as well as I that it's a charade. My daughter nailed it once when she asked, "I know you have a hip implant, but why are they searching you?"

In the last two years, I've flown from Stockholm, London, Moscow, Tokyo, Johannesburg, Port-au-Prince, and Copenhagen. I have never been searched to the degree that the woman in Springfield, Missouri, carried out on my t-shirt and summer skirt–clad, flip-flop-wearing body. Overseas they seem to do a bit of sensible profiling at the border, and once I explain my hip replacement and they do a minimal search, I'm generally free to go.

Which brings me to the body scanners. They are time saving, efficient, and not nearly as invasive. I worship them. They are freedom from the pointless ritual of lifting up my shirt, turning down my waistband, justifying my lingerie, and explaining for the thousandth time to a federal employee why I had a hip replacement at 45. If the TSA is going to make security a humiliating but necessary ordeal, I say, get it over with fast.

> *"Because the screener(s) doing the search cannot look for someone who actually might pose a threat, screening zero-risk fliers makes everyone else less safe."*

Passenger Screening Policies Are Misguided and Ineffective

John C. Wohlstetter

John C. Wohlstetter is a blogger, author, and senior fellow at the Discovery Institute. In the following viewpoint, he derides Transportation Security Administration (TSA) passenger screening strategies as wrongheaded because screeners search zero-risk passengers instead of focusing on high-risk passengers. Wohlstetter believes this approach doesn't make any sense and proposes that the TSA emulate the Israeli system, which screens for suspicious behavior and high-risk profiles. To do this, he says, Americans must reject concerns about political correctness, hire TSA employees that have experience evaluating risk, and give specialty training to those hires.

As you read, consider the following questions:

1. How does Wohlstetter describe the TSA position that once screening is started a passenger cannot refuse to complete the process?

2. What groups does the author believe would never have made it on planes if the United States employed an Israeli-style passenger screening system?

3. What does Wohlstetter call Lanny Davis's statement that he feels safer as a flier when he is searched?

As public outrage grows over the Transportation Security [Administration's (TSA's)] new, more aggressive screening procedures—scanners that reveal body silhouettes, aggressive pat downs touching intimate body parts—the reasons why travelers are upset need to be examined, and better ways found to protect us.

First let's find the rules, or can we? TSA's "For Travelers" website sub-page shows no hint of what lies in store for passengers. TSA rules are in their "Research Center" sub-page. Trolling through various headings and sub-menus yielded no guidance whatsoever. Not that you are safe being unable to find the rules. TSA has a standard line of defense available to any regulatory body: the ancient maxim that ignorance of the law is no excuse. It dates from when laws were rules everyone knew: do not kill the king, violate the queen, desecrate the church, steal your neighbor's land or his cow. The modern regulatory state gives us tens of thousands of pages of statutes and regulations enacted pursuant to complex, barely readable laws. Not even attorneys general or Supreme Court justices can know more than a tiny fraction of the whole. Yet the maxim stands, a monument to how fiction trumps reality in today's byzantine legal maze.

The Bargain After 9/11

The original post–Sept. 11 [referring to the terrorist attacks on the United States on September 11, 2001, also known as 9/11] bargain was this: A passenger may refuse security screening upon deciding not to board a plane. The position taken now by TSA is that once screening is started a passenger cannot refuse to complete the process. *This is, put simply, bait and switch.* It is a bureaucracy's attempt to circumvent this fundamental rule adopted after 9/11; screeners frequently advise passengers step-by-step, so that the process gets started innocently and then turns ugly later. Threatening someone who demurs in midstream with a large fine plus prosecution is bad enough; holding someone after screening stops without legal cause to do so is false imprisonment, a tort (civil wrong) actionable in court. It is also a violation of federally created statutory civil rights, and creates a right to file a civil lawsuit against federal or state officers who violate civil rights.

Israeli security neither uses body scanners nor intimate cringe-inducing pat downs. The former do not detect certain explosives and critics say radiation exposure is low only if they are properly operated, not a given with TSA drones who are hardly radiologists at Johns Hopkins. As for pat downs, patting down a screaming infant or trembling mom or an embarrassed grandfather makes no one safe. *Searching zero-risk passengers makes no one safer.* Indeed, because the screener(s) doing the search cannot look for someone who actually might pose a threat, screening zero-risk fliers makes everyone else *less safe.*

I would take the scanner over having my privates patted; I pity anyone who gets jollies from seeing an outline of my dilapidated carcass on the threshold of my golden years. Are body-cavity searches next, with terrorists already emulating drug mules? Shall we deputize every screener as airport proctologists?

A Better Way

There is a far better way than TSA's to deal with security threats: Israel's way. Israeli security screeners are smart people who look courteously for terrorists, without political correctness; our screeners are dumb people who look, often rudely, for things and bow to political correctness. Israel profiles by behavior; we prattle on about equal treatment regardless of

Tired of being slowed down at airport security, Vince began to travel in only a pair of Speedos.

"Tired of Being Slowed Down at Airport Security ...," cartoon by John McPherson, www.CartoonStock.com.

risk profile. News reports say that Homeland Insecurity Secretary Janet "the System Worked" Napolitano is on the verge of exempting Muslim women from certain screening and patdown procedures, while Christian, Jewish, Buddhist and secular women must endure.

The Christmas 2009 underwear bomber with the unpronounceable name would never have gotten within a mile of an El Al [Israel Airlines] plane. Nor would the 9/11 terrorists have made it on board in Israel—or gotten past an El Al desk in America. While America singles out Muslim sensibilities for special treatment—members of the very group from which most terrorists come (yes, we all know that most Muslims are not terrorists)—Israel singles out security threats by assessing individual risk.

Thursday night [in November 2010], former [president] Bill Clinton flack Lanny Davis said on *Hannity* [a conservative TV show] that he feels safer as a flier when he is searched: a noble proposition—and on its face a preposterous one. Put simply, Lanny Davis is a zero-risk passenger. Davis said he had watched the late Sen. Daniel Patrick Moynihan being patted down. The late Sen. Edward Kennedy was on a no-fly list for months, amusing Republicans surely, but hardly making us more secure.

Fixing the Security Mess

How to fix this mess? First, look for people, not things. Second, throw out political correctness and begin profiling by behavior—not ethnicity. Third, hire people who have put their lives on the line—literally—evaluating suspect risk, and lived to tell their stories, not would-be bureaucrats who stare at screens and risk sore backsides. Soldiers and cops are good hires; paper pushers and janitors are not. Give specialty training to people who are smart, skilled, and willing to supplement rule guidelines with independent, intelligent, and instant on-the-spot judgment; do not waste time giving basic training to unskilled dolts who will mechanically apply rigid rules no matter how manifestly absurd the real-life situation. Oh, and please fire the jerks who reduce infants to tears, force a developmentally disabled child to shuck his leg braces and walk through unaided, shout at pregnant moms, etc.

Over the years, repeated tests by teams posing as passengers have shown that contraband, including weapons, can be successfully smuggled aboard aircraft, fooling metal detectors and TSA screeners. We fly safer today because cabin doors are locked and not to be opened, because the Todd Beamer [passenger on United Airlines Flight 93 who attempted to stop the hijacking of that flight on September 11, 2001] "Let's roll!" protocol is followed by passengers, because air marshals fly with us and because of far better luggage screening. Abusing the sensibilities of passengers is unnecessary, cruel and adds zero to security. And if my privates are to be touched, let it be by someone I choose, not in public and not by a drone at TSA.

> "Random screenings not based on risk assessments misdirect the screening process and add to the indignity of travel."

The Transportation Security Administration's Intrusions Undermine Security

Rand Paul

Rand Paul is a Republican senator from Kentucky. In the following viewpoint, he criticizes the Transportation Security Administration (TSA) for being unreasonable and excessive during an incident at the airport in which he refused to undergo an invasive pat down by security. Paul contends that the TSA violated his civil liberties by harassing him and forcing him to undergo an ineffective and invasive physical search without a warrant. He argues that it would spare travelers frustration and indignity if the TSA focused on intelligence and police work instead of compromising the civil liberties of all passengers.

As you read, consider the following questions:

1. According to Paul, where did they detain him after he refused a pat down at the airport?

2. According to Paul, how did TSA director John S. Pistole justify the invasive search of a six-year-old girl in Bowling Green, Kentucky?

3. What constitutional amendment does Paul believe that the TSA is violating?

Today [in January 2012], while en route to Washington to speak to hundreds of thousands of people at the March for Life, I was detained by the Transportation Security Administration (TSA) for not agreeing to a pat down after an irregularity was found in my full-body scan. Despite removing my belt, glasses, wallet and shoes, the scanner and TSA also wanted my dignity. I refused.

I showed them the potentially offending part of my body, my leg. They were not interested. They wanted to touch me and to pat me down. I requested to be re-scanned. They refused and detained me in a 10-foot-by-10-foot area reserved for potential terrorists.

I told them that I was a frequent flier and that just days ago I was allowed to be re-scanned when the scanner made an error. At no time did I ask for special treatment, but I did insist that all travelers be awarded some decency and leniency in accommodating the screening process.

My detention was real and I was repeatedly instructed not to leave the holding area. When I used my phone to inform my office that I would miss my flight, and thus miss my speech at the March for Life, I was told that now I would be subjected to a full-body pat down.

I asked if I could simply restart the screening process to show that the machine had made an error. I was denied and informed that since I used my phone, to call for help, I must now submit or not fly.

Let me be clear: I neither asked for nor expect any special treatment for being a U.S. senator. In fact, this case is not about me at all. This is about every single one of us and how we are sick of the intrusive nature of our government.

While sitting in the cubicle, I thought to myself, have the terrorists won? Have we sacrificed our liberty and our dignity for security? Finally, the airport head of TSA arrived after I had missed my flight. He let me go back through the scanner and this time the scanner did not go off. The only comment from TSA was that some of the alarms are simply random.

So passengers who do everything right, remove their belts, remove their wallets, remove their shoes, their glasses and all of the contents in their pockets are then subjected to random pat downs and tricked into believing that the scanners actually detected something.

I have been through some of this with TSA director John S. Pistole before. Last spring, a 6-year-old girl from Bowling Green was subjected to an invasive search despite her parent's objections. Mr. Pistole claimed that small children were indeed a risk because a girl in Kandahar, Afghanistan, had exploded a bomb in a market in Afghanistan. But Mr. Pistole, this girl wasn't from Kandahar and she wasn't in Afghanistan. Isn't there a significant difference?

In writing, he replied that TSA concluded because a child in a market in Afghanistan exploded a bomb, all American children needed to be evaluated as potential threats. My response: If you treat everyone equally as a potential threat, then you direct much attention to those who are never going to attack us and spend less time with those whose risk profiles indicate a need for tougher screening.

Random screenings not based on risk assessments misdirect the screening process and add to the indignity of travel. Those passengers who suffer through the process of partially disrobing should be rewarded with less invasive examination.

Ever since the news of my struggle with TSA, the phones in my office have been ringing off the hook with calls from citizens who sympathize with my frustration, as they, too, feel

How to Opt Out of the Body-Scanning Process

You can tell the TSA [Transportation Security Administration] agent that you do not wish to go through the scanner. TSA agents are required under TSA policy to honor your request, but might try to encourage or pressure you to go through anyway. To be as clear as possible, say, "I opt out." However, you should know that if you opt out, you will be subject to a pat down that many people find as or more troubling than the body scanner. You also have the right to opt your children out of the scan.

American Civil Liberties Union,
"Know Your Rights When Traveling," ACLU.org, 2012.

their liberties are being compromised every time they travel. My office is being inundated with their stories of assault and harassment by TSA agents. This agency's disregard for our civil liberties is something we are expected to understand and accept. But we are tired of being insulted and we are tired of having our dignity compromised. TSA was created in the aftermath of the Sept. 11 [2001] terrorist attacks, but was it necessary? Has it overstepped its bounds? Is it respecting the rights of citizens?

It is time for us to question the effectiveness of TSA. America can prosper, preserve personal liberty and repel national security threats without intruding into the personal lives of its citizens.

Every time we travel, we are expected to surrender our Fourth Amendment rights, yet willingly giving up our rights does not make us any safer. It is infuriating that this agency feels entitled to revoke our civil liberties while doing little to keep us safe.

Is the TSA looking at flight manifests? Are we researching those boarding the planes? Are we targeting or looking at those who might attack us? Apparently not, if we are wasting our time patting down 6-year-old girls.

If a federally funded TSA is going to exist, then its focus should be on police work and it must respect the rights of citizens. The TSA should not universally insult all travelers; it should however research, track, monitor and target people that are, in fact, threats to our nation.

This blatant violation of the Fourth Amendment, which protects Americans against unwarranted search and seizure, has insulted many citizens, and rightfully so. I, along with many other travelers, do not view traveling as a crime that warrants government search and seizure. In fact, I view traveling as a basic right, for Americans are free to travel from state to state as they please.

I refused an unnecessary pat down and stood up for my rights as an American citizen. This is a battle Americans face every time they fly. It is my firm belief that TSA should not have such broad authority to violate our constitutional rights in ineffective and invasive physical searches, thus I will further push for the reinstatement of traveler privacy and rights. I will be proposing legislation that will allow for adults to be rescreened if they so choose.

> *"AIT [advanced imaging technology]
> represents the very latest in passenger
> screening technological advancement
> and addresses a broad range of threats,
> many of which cannot be addressed by
> older technologies like metal detectors."*

The Passenger Screening System Protects Americans' Civil Rights and Civil Liberties

Robin Kane and Lee Kair

Robin Kane is the assistant administrator for operational process and technology at the Transportation Security Administration (TSA) and Lee Kair is the assistant administrator for security operations at the TSA. In the following viewpoint, they empha-size the effectiveness and safety of advanced imaging technology (AIT) and state that it is a paramount goal of the TSA to pro-tect passenger privacy. Kane and Kair point out that strict safe-guards have been put in place to ensure that the body-scanner images cannot be stored or printed and are maintained on the monitor for a very short time. Furthermore, they assert, new

Robin Kane and Lee Kair, Statement Before the United States House of Representatives Committee on Oversight and Government Reform, Subcommittee on National Security, Homeland Defense, and Foreign Operations, March 16, 2011.

technologies such as automatic target recognition (ATR) enhance passenger privacy by eliminating passenger-specific images and focusing only on areas that show an anomaly.

As you read, consider the following questions:

1. According to Kane and Kair, how many AIT machines does the TSA want to deploy by the end of 2012?

2. What do the authors say is equivalent to the radiation of a single AIT screening?

3. According to a number of polls cited in the viewpoint, what percentage of Americans accept AIT technology?

Working in concert with our international, federal, state, local, tribal, territorial, and private sector partners, TSA's [Transportation Security Administration's] mission is to prevent terrorist attacks and reduce the vulnerability of the nation's transportation system to terrorism. AIT [advanced imaging technology] is a powerful advancement in our continuing effort to improve aviation security, which also includes work with the law enforcement and intelligence communities, strengthening supply chain security, and increased international cooperation. While we have made significant advances in reducing the threat to aviation security, al-Qaeda and other terrorist organizations remain intent upon attacking the aviation system. We have witnessed the evolution of this threat from checked baggage, to carry-on baggage, and now to air cargo and nonmetallic explosives hidden on the body.

One of the most salient examples is the bombing plot by al-Qaeda in the Arabian Peninsula resulting in the December 25, 2009, alleged attempt by Umar Farouk Abdulmutallab to blow up a U.S.-flagged airplane en route to Detroit using a nonmetallic explosive device that was not and could not have been discovered by a metal detector.

TSA works diligently to protect and secure the U.S. transportation domain against the evolving threat as terrorists adapt their tactics to attempt to circumvent our technology and procedures. We continue to modernize our technology deployments, including AIT. We have deployed nearly 500 AIT machines at domestic airports throughout the country to enhance security by safely screening passengers for metallic and nonmetallic weapons and explosives—including objects concealed under layers of clothing, while protecting the privacy of the traveler. We have also deployed new portable explosive trace detection machines, advanced technology X-ray systems, and bottled liquid scanners to enhance our security technology in the aviation domain.

We also have deployed additional behavior detection officers, federal air marshals and explosives-detection canine teams at airports throughout the country. Nearly a year ago, in April 2010, we implemented new, enhanced security measures for all air carriers with international flights to the U.S. that use real-time, threat-based intelligence to better mitigate the evolving terrorist threat. Last November [2010], we achieved a major aviation security milestone: 100 percent of passengers on flights within or bound for the United States are now checked by TSA against government watch lists through the Secure Flight program, as recommended in *The 9/11 Commission Report* [formally known as the *Final Report of the National Commission on Terrorist Attacks Upon the United States*].

AIT Is Effective at Detecting Metallic and Nonmetallic Threat Items

AIT represents the very latest in passenger screening technological advancement and addresses a broad range of threats, many of which cannot be addressed by older technologies like metal detectors. TSA's work with AIT began in 2007 and has included testing and evaluation in both the laboratory and in airports. Our extensive experience with AIT has made us the world leader in its implementation in the aviation environment. The agency tested and piloted the use of AIT at several airports around the country prior to the December 2009 attempted attack. As a result, TSA was able to accelerate AIT deployment following the incident to enable our transportation security officers to quickly and effectively detect metallic and nonmetallic threat items.

Based upon our analysis of the latest intelligence and after studying available technologies and other processes, TSA has concluded AIT is an effective method to detect threat items concealed on passengers while maintaining efficient checkpoint screening operations. Accordingly, in January 2010, TSA determined that AIT should be deployed as part of its primary screening program. TSA continually evaluates these technologies, their software, and associated screening procedures to ensure that they are effective against established and anticipated threats while continuing to protect passenger privacy, civil rights, and civil liberties.

TSA's goal is to deploy nearly 1,275 AIT machines by the end of calendar year 2012, providing AIT coverage at more than half our operational screening lanes. The ability to deploy AIT to airports and the number of machines deployed are directly affected by the amount of funding and available resources. Accordingly, the president's budget request for FY [fiscal year] 2012 includes approximately $105.2 million in base and additional funding to continue deployment of AIT.

AIT Is a Safe and Reliable Screening Method

The safety of the traveling public is TSA's number one priority. Our technology policies require compliance with consensus-based scientific safety standards including those administered by the Health Physics Society and accredited by the American National Standards Institute for screening equipment using ionizing radiation.

AIT machines are safe and efficient. The radiation dose from backscatter AIT machines has been independently evalu-

What Is Advanced Image Technology?

Strict privacy safeguards are built into the foundation of TSA's [the Transportation Security Administration's] use of advanced imaging technology [AIT] to protect passenger privacy and ensure anonymity. . . .

TSA recently installed new software on all millimeter wave imaging technology machines—upgrades designed to enhance privacy by eliminating passenger-specific images and instead auto-detecting potential threats and indicating their location on a generic outline of a person. Areas identified as containing potential threats will require additional screening. . . .

By eliminating the image of an actual passenger and replacing it with a generic outline of a person, passengers are able to view the same outline that the TSA officer sees. . . .

For units that do not yet have the new software, TSA has taken all efforts to ensure passenger privacy. To that end, the officer who assists the passenger never sees the image the technology produces and the officer who views the image is remotely located in a secure resolution room and never sees the passenger. The two officers communicate via wireless headset.

Advanced imaging technology cannot store, print, transmit or save the image, and the image is automatically deleted from the system after it is cleared by the remotely located security officer. Officers evaluating images are not permitted to take cameras, cell phones or photoenabled devices into the resolution room. To further protect passenger privacy, backscatter technology has privacy filters that blur images.

Transportation Security Administration, "Privacy: Advanced Image Technology," TSA.gov, 2012.

ated by the Food and Drug Administration, the National Institute of Standards and Technology, and the Johns Hopkins University Applied Physics Laboratory, all of which have affirmed that the systems comply with established standards for safety. Public versions of our safety testing reports are available on TSA's website at www.tsa.gov.

A single screening using backscatter technology produces a radiation dose equivalent to approximately two minutes of flying on an airplane at a cruising altitude of 30,000 feet. Millimeter wave technology does not emit ionizing radiation and instead uses radio frequency energy. The energy projected by these units is a fraction of other commercially approved radio frequency devices, such as cell phones and two-way radios.

TSA is sensitive to the needs of all types of travelers. For example, transportation security officers (TSOs) are trained to work with parents to ensure a respectful screening process for the entire family while providing the best possible security for all travelers. TSA never separates a child from the adult accompanying him or her, and the adult traveling with the child observes the entire screening process. AIT is safe for children, and children of all ages may undergo screening using AIT as long as they are able to stand with their hands above their head for the five to seven seconds needed to conduct the scan.

AIT Procedures Protect Passenger Privacy, Civil Rights, and Civil Liberties

Strict safeguards to protect passenger privacy and ensure anonymity have been put in place by TSA as it has deployed AIT. The machines deployed by TSA at airports cannot store or print passenger images, and images are maintained on the monitor only for as long as it takes to resolve any anomalies. Images from TSA screening operations cannot be, have not been, and are not retained for any purpose.

Further, TSOs reviewing the image are unable to see the individual undergoing screening, and a TSO screening the passenger cannot see the image. AIT machines do not produce photographic-quality images that would permit recognition of the person screened. A facial blur has also been applied to both the millimeter wave and backscatter technologies.

The Department of Homeland Security's (DHS's) chief privacy officer has conducted a privacy impact assessment of the AIT machines and updated those assessments as the program has developed. The full results of that assessment are available to the public on the Privacy Office's website at www.dhs.gov/privacy. TSA's screening protocols ensure that such screening does not unreasonably intrude on a passenger's privacy in the airport environment and that the public's privacy concerns related to AIT screening are adequately addressed. According to our statistics, more than 98 percent of individuals selected for AIT screening have opted to be screened by this technology over other screening methods such as a pat down. In addition, there have been a number of public polls indicating public acceptance of the technology at nearly 80 percent. TSA provides notice to the public of the use of the AIT machines prior to the passenger's entering the machine. The notice also advises the individual that they may decline AIT screening and be screened by a pat down instead.

In Case of an Anomaly

If an anomaly is discovered by the TSO operating the AIT machine, TSA procedures require TSOs to use additional inspection methods to determine whether the anomaly is a threat. These methods may include visual inspection, swabbing for explosives, or a pat down to resolve the anomaly.

TSA has been working to ensure passengers' civil rights and civil liberties are also protected. We are pursuing technology enhancements, such as automatic target recognition, which we will discuss in more detail shortly, to enhance passenger privacy. Additionally, TSA and other DHS outreach and privacy offices have conducted extensive outreach to communities representing persons with disabilities and special medical needs, as well as major medical centers, to discuss AIT and other challenges encountered by members of these communities during the screening process. We will continue to work with these communities to make refinements and adjustments to our screening protocols that are respectful of the needs of these individuals while ensuring the security of the traveling public. This collaboration has already resulted in refinements. For example, TSA has developed a notification card to allow passengers with disabilities to communicate discreetly to a TSO that they have a condition or disability that might affect their screening.

Field Testing of Automatic Target Recognition (ATR)

While we are rapidly deploying AIT machines to U.S. airports, we also are exploring enhancements to this technology to further address privacy issues and civil rights and civil liberties concerns. Specifically, TSA is field testing auto-detection software, referred to as automatic target recognition (ATR), which enhances passenger privacy by eliminating passenger-specific images and instead highlighting the area with a detected anomaly on a generic outline of a person. Pat downs used to resolve such anomalies will be limited to the areas of the body displaying an alarm unless the number of anomalies detected requires a full-body pat down. If no anomalies are detected, the screen displays the word "OK" with no icon. With ATR, the screen will be located on the outside of the machine and can be viewed by the TSO and the passenger.

As with current AIT software, ATR-enabled units deployed at airports are not capable of storing or printing images. This software eliminates the need for a TSO to view passenger images in a separate room because no actual image of the passenger is produced, reducing associated staffing and construction costs. ATR software represents a substantial step forward in addressing passenger privacy concerns while maintaining TSA's standards for detection. TSA plans to continually update and test enhanced versions of the software in order to ensure that technology with the highest detection standards is in use.

> *"Conservative and Orthodox rabbis have voiced concern over the scanners, and in some cases they've requested compromises to ensure that their modesty concerns are met."*

Passenger Screening Policies Violate Religious Modesty

Josh Nathan-Kazis

Josh Nathan-Kazis is a reporter for the Jewish Daily Forward. *In the following viewpoint, he reports that leaders in both Conservative and Orthodox Jewish communities have expressed strong concerns over the use of full-body scanners at US airports, arguing that these new security procedures violate Jewish laws of modesty. Nathan-Kazis finds that many of these leaders are requesting compromises to reconcile religious law with practical concerns of security. One possible solution, Nathan-Kazis notes, is making sure the scanners block out the faces of passengers as well as certain private body parts to protect modesty.*

As you read, consider the following questions:

1. How do millimeter wave scanners work, according to Nathan-Kazis?

2. How does Nathan-Kazis describe the Jewish principle of *pikuach nefesh*?

3. What other religious group does the author say has raised concerns over the full-body scanners?

Observant Jews are voicing concerns over modesty and looking for compromise on the Transportation Security Administration's [TSA's] plan to expand the use of whole-body imaging machines for airport security, after last month's [in December 2009] failed attempt to bomb a Detroit-bound jetliner.

Jewish Laws of *Tzniut*

Leaders in both Conservative and Orthodox communities are debating how scanners with the ability to see through clothing intersect with Jewish laws of *tzniut* [also *tseniut*], or modesty, which are observed differently among denominations but generally require Jews to cover their bodies.

"It creates a tension between the Jewish value of protecting lives, which is very strong, and the Jewish value of modesty for women and for men," said David Rosenn, a Conservative rabbi and the executive director of Avodah, a Jewish service program.

Body Scanners

The full-body scanners actually come in two varieties, each using a different type of technology. Millimeter wave scanners use radio frequency beams to create a 3-D image of the body. Backscatter X-rays use small amounts of radiation to create 2-D images of each side of the body. Both result in sketchy digital representations of the naked body of the person being scanned, allowing screeners to see items concealed under clothing.

There are currently 74 full-body scanning machines in operation at American airports. The TSA, which oversees airport

The Philosophy of *Tseniut*

The Talmud and later rabbinic literature provide additional material relating to sexual conduct in general, and *tseniut* (modesty) in particular. An aim of *tseniut* [also *tzniut*] is to diminish the possibility of improper sexual temptations that could lead to sinful behavior. The human sexual drive is quite powerful, and the *tseniut* laws are intended to keep that drive under control.

Tseniut, though, is not simply a system of prevention from sin. Rather, it encompasses a positive philosophy relating to the nature of human beings. While acknowledging the power of human sexuality, *tseniut* teaches that human beings are more than mere sexual beings.

In his famous book, *I and Thou*, the philosopher Martin Buber pointed out that ideal human relationships involve mutual knowledge and respect, where people treat themselves and others as valuable persons—not as things. *Tseniut*, in fact, seeks to foster the highest form of I-thou relationship. By insisting on modest dress and behavior, the laws of *tseniut* promote a framework for human relationships that transcends the physical/sexual aspects.

Marc D. Angel,
"Rethinking Jewish Law's Call for Female Modesty,"
FailedMessiah.com, February 15, 2012.

security throughout the country, recently announced that 150 more backscatter X-rays will be put to use early this year.

According to the TSA's website, images from the backscatter X-rays are processed through an algorithm meant to protect the privacy of the passenger. The images are viewed by TSA officers who sit at terminals behind closed doors and have no personal interaction with the people being scanned. "They're just spending 10 seconds or so looking at the image to make sure there aren't any concealed threat items," said Ann Davis, a spokeswoman for the TSA. "Then the image gets deleted."

Davis said that the officers reviewing the scan would not necessarily be the same gender as the individual being scanned.

Raising Concerns

Conservative and Orthodox rabbis have voiced concern over the scanners, and in some cases they've requested compromises to ensure that their modesty concerns are met. Last June, the Washington office of Agudath Israel [of America], which represents traditional American Orthodox communities, sent a letter to a Senate subcommittee reviewing a TSA-related bill, promoting an amendment to the House version of the bill that limited the use of the full-body scanners to situations in which passengers had already failed a metal detector test, and which would require that those passengers be offered the option of a pat down search.

"As an organization that represents observant Jews, Agudath Israel finds [full-body imaging] to be offensive, demeaning, and far short of acceptable norms of modesty under the laws and practices of Judaism and many faith communities," the letter read.

Abba Cohen, the rabbi who directs Agudath Israel's Washington office, said in an interview that it is important that the full-body scans be adopted with care, if they are adopted at all. "In the rush to move to full-body scans, there hasn't been any kind of process of determining under what circumstances these scans could and should be used," Cohen said.

Compromise?

Still, Avi Shafran, a spokesman for Agudath Israel, made it clear that his organization saw room for compromise. "Orthodox Jewish men and women go to doctors," Shafran said. "Because it's a professional environment, and that person is doing this because of his job, what would be a violation of modesty in one circumstance is not in a medical circumstance. That could be utilized here."

Other rabbis emphasized the importance of the Jewish principle of *pikuach nefesh*, or the saving of human life. "We have a responsibility to make sure that we are protected and to guarantee our physical security, or else our capacity to serve as ambassadors of God in this world is impossible," said Kenneth Brander, dean of Yeshiva University's Center for the Jewish Future. "That being said . . . the same way that if someone can save oneself on the Sabbath without violating the Sabbath, one does so, if we can figure out ways so that [the full-body scanner] not only blocks out the face, but perhaps certain private parts are shaded in ways that do not compromise security but protect modesty, I think that's something we should [support]."

Other Religious Groups' Objections

The scanners have raised concerns outside the American Jewish community as well. In early January, a group of European rabbis issued a press release voicing distress over the scanners. And in the United States, American Muslim groups have said that the scans may violate their religion's standards of modesty. "The Prophet Muhammad, peace be upon him, said every faith has an intrinsic character, and the intrinsic character of Islam is modesty," said Ibrahim Hooper, a spokesman for the Council on American-Islamic Relations, which is a Washington-based civil rights and advocacy group. "We have specific requirements for what can be exposed of the body, both for men and women, and needless to say, having a nude image displayed on a screen is not something we appreciate in religious terms."

Hooper said that it was important to his organization that the full-body scans remain one option. "I think in the Muslim community it's one topic of discussion," he said. "People are deciding what they are going to do. Am I going to cut down on my traveling? Am I going to grit my teeth and go through it? Am I going to object? And then if I object, what's going to happen?"

According to Mary Boys, a professor at Union Theological Seminary, the body scanners don't seem to have raised widespread concerns among Christians. "I don't see that this is going to come up as a theological issue among a lot of Christian groups," Boys said.

Periodical and Internet Sources Bibliography

The following articles have been selected to supplement the diverse views presented in this chapter.

Locke Bowman	"Airport Security: For What It's Worth," *Huffington Post*, June 27, 2011.
Grand Rapids Press	"New Airport Body Scanners Necessary Tool in Fight Against Terrorism," August 25, 2010.
Gene Healy	"Hassling the Innocent Is TSA's Specialty," *DC Examiner*, January 29, 2012.
Kevin Huffman	"How Much Will We Do to Ensure the Terrorists Don't Win?," *PostPartisan* (blog), *Washington Post*, November 19, 2010.
Darrell Issa	"Less Privacy, No Added Security," *National Review Online*, December 6, 2010.
Thomas E. McNamara	"To Find the Needles, Reduce the Haystack," *Los Angeles Times*, November 21, 2010.
Joanna Molloy	"Rant on Airport Security 'Groin Check' Goes Viral, but Curb the Outrage—Safety Is at Stake," *New York Daily News*, November 16, 2010.
Janet Napolitano	"Napolitano: Scanners Are Safe, Pat-Downs Discreet," *USA Today*, November 14, 2010.
David Rittgers	"Body Scanners: The Naked Truth," *New York Post*, November 17, 2010.
Michael Scott	"First a Hand on Your Crotch, Next a Boot in Your Face," *CounterPunch*, November 24, 2010.
Adam Serwer	"Why We Are Angry at the TSA," *American Prospect*, November 17, 2010.

CHAPTER 3

Should Profiling Be Used as a Security Strategy?

Chapter Preface

In recent years, a number of American commentators and officials have advocated for a more effective airport security strategy. Frustrated by the Transportation Security Administration's (TSA's) screening process, which forces travelers to take off their shoes and endure invasive pat downs and/or mandatory body scans, many policy makers have turned their eyes to Israel's efficient airport security system. According to many security experts, Israel has the most effective method of screening airline passengers in the world—and Israeli airport security officers don't make passengers take off their shoes or endure full-body scans. At the nation's largest airport, Ben Gurion International Airport, more than one million people pass through the airport each month. Yet no flight from that airport has ever been hijacked, and the airport has not been attacked since 1972. Considering the threats it faces, it is an impressive security accomplishment. The TSA has long been interested in adopting Israeli methods to improve America's airport security.

Israel's airport security strategy evolved as a reaction to the high level of threats it faced on a constant basis. A focal point of Islamic fundamentalist and other radical terrorist groups, Israel has been forced to adapt to a hostile environment to protect its airports and airline industry. On May 31, 1972, terrorists from the Japanese Red Army attacked the Ben Gurion airport outside of Tel Aviv with machine guns. Twenty-six people died in the attack and seventy-six were wounded. On December 27, 1985, terrorists simultaneously attacked the ticket counter of El Al Israel Airlines in Rome and Vienna using machine guns and grenades. Nineteen people were killed and many wounded. In 1986 a security screener at an Israeli airport found a suitcase full of explosives in the terminal. Thirteen people were injured when the bomb detonated. As a frequent target of terrorist groups, Israel had to develop an airport security strategy that worked.

Israel's solution to its airport security issue is a sophisticated system of intelligence reporting, racial and ethnic profiling, and state-of-the-art technology for detecting advanced explosives and weapons. Israeli security agents focus on "the human factor," using their eyes and instincts to detect lies and deceptive behavior. All passengers undergo a twenty-five-second interview in which security agents ask why a passenger has come to the airport, where he or she has been and is going, and the person's general background. Any inconsistency in a passenger's answer will trigger a more rigorous investigation. According to Pini Schiff, the former head of security at Ben Gurion airport, "your aim is to locate, to find the one passenger that is a terrorist and is carrying explosive material under his possession. You have to characterize the passengers and to focus on those who are suspected and it's less than one percent."

Racial and ethnic profiling is central to Israeli passenger screening. That means certain ethnicities or nationalities will immediately trigger more intensive screening, such as people of Palestinian descent, or young Muslim men. Although Israeli security experts argue that not every Muslim man sends up a red flag at airport screening checkpoints, critics of Israeli security contend that the system blatantly harasses and singles out young Muslim men.

Ariel Merari, a noted Israeli terrorism expert, contends such a strategy is common sense. He maintains that "it would be foolish not to use profiling when everyone knows that most terrorists come from certain ethnic groups. They are likely to be Muslim and young, and the potential threat justifies inconveniencing a certain ethnic group."

In the United States, racial and ethnic profiling is a complicated and controversial security strategy that many Americans are not willing to adopt. However, a substantial group of

Americans view it as a more effective way to identify possible terrorists than the current screening system employed in US airports. The debate over adopting Israeli security methods—including profiling—is the focus of the following chapter. Other viewpoints explore the role of political correctness in the US airport security strategy and the importance of intelligence and investigation in protecting the US aviation industry.

> *"The hard question is to figure out how to profile. And one key element is to be sensitive of the needs of those individuals who are members of the targeted races and nationalities."*

Profiling Should Be Used as a Security Strategy

Richard A. Epstein

Richard A. Epstein is an author, educator, and senior fellow at the Hoover Institution. In the following viewpoint, he suggests that the main problems of the Transportation Security Administration (TSA) lie with its policies on profiling and unionizing its employees. Epstein argues that the TSA employing racial and ethnic profiling within reason as part of an effective passenger screening strategy is constitutional and practical considering the threats the United States faces. He proposes that the TSA look to the Israeli system for elements that would work in America. It is key, he maintains, that any profiling strategy be sensitive and respectful to individuals who belong to targeted racial and ethnic groups.

As you read, consider the following questions:

1. What is "blob" technology, according to Epstein?

2. How many daily flights does Epstein say there are in Israel?

3. How many flights does Epstein say come out of the United States every day?

On December 4, 2010, John [S.] Pistole, the new head of the Transportation Security Administration (TSA), gave an extensive interview to Matthew Kaminski of the *Wall Street Journal.* The interview took place at an "[u]ndisclosed location near Washington," from which Pistole has doubtless departed. But if his whereabouts are a great mystery, as befits a man who is knee-deep in security matters, his policy directions are plain to see. They compromise a mix of the good, the bad, and the ugly. The question is how to disentangle the parts.

The Good News and the Bad News

The best news comes from his clear recognition that technological improvements can go a long way to reduce the inevitable conflicts between liberty and security. To no one's surprise, these tensions have become more intense with the TSA's decision to give all airline passengers the unappetizing choice between intrusive full-body screening machines and offensive personal pat downs.

The bad news is that though Pistole speaks favorably of this much-needed technology, acquiring that technology in the immediate future seems unlikely. For instance, Pistole refers to a "blob" technology, currently in place in Amsterdam, which can pick out foreign objects on a person without giving detailed images of everyone's private parts to the body scanners. The obvious question is why that technology is not also in place in the United States, or at least in certain airports, like Detroit's, that seem to pose the highest risk for hostile action. In a nation that spends billions of dollars on misguided stimulus programs, here is one needed public expenditure that should rise to the top of the list.

The Threat of Unionization

Budgeting for much-needed technology will not grow any likelier if Pistole implements the truly ugly: the unionization of 55,000 TSA employees, which may be just around the corner. To be sure, our misguided head of TSA utters soothing words in the *Wall Street Journal*: recognition of unions will come only with certain conditions. Most importantly, he says, the unions will not be able to strike, nor will they be allowed to engage in any activities with an adverse impact on security.

These familiar bromides are, of course, a recipe for a disaster. Last I looked, no public unions have ever bargained for wage cuts in order to boost national security. Today, all sorts of public employees are not allowed to strike, but that has not prevented them from ringing up huge gains in wages, working conditions, retirement benefits, and health care. Compulsory arbitration, about which Pistole is mum, is the inevitable quid pro quo [something given for something else] for surrendering the right to strike, which public employees should never be allowed to exercise in the first place.

This pattern has been repeated countless times with public unions at the state and federal levels. If the police, firefighters, and prison guards have never let public health and security get in the way of their own economic advancement, what makes anyone think that this ugly and inexcusable maneuver will be any different?

The consequences for public safety and comfort are dire. The TSA's budget should be spent, among other things, on improved scanning technology, but instead the money may make its way into the hands of TSA workers, who will gladly accept a bit more public abuse in exchange for a thicker pay packet. The choice between better scanners and TSA unions is a no-brainer. Rather than let the TSA imitate the unionized Post Office, the Post Office should imitate the currently non-unionized TSA.

With private unemployment rates as high as they are, there is no need to offer unionization to enlist new workers into the TSA's ranks. But in Pistole's unfortunate riff, we hear once again the misguided voice of President [Barack] Obama, whose blind fealty to union interests has marred his entire career in public office.

The Issue of Profiling

Pistole's interview also addressed broader questions of airport security, and there is more good news here. Pistole is to be commended for noting that monitoring ordinary passengers in security lines is only a small part of the overall task. It is also critical to do lots of surveillance of individuals who should never be allowed to get within a mile of an airport gate to begin with.

Flying secret agents on airplanes and positioning uniformed officers at key locations—both of which seem to be critical to any decent security strategy—are essential pieces of the overall plan. The less we hear about these details in public, the better we all are, so long as we are confident that some coherent program is in place.

The most contentious issue Pistole has to face, however, is the distasteful but unavoidable question of racial profiling. According to the *Wall Street Journal* interview, Pistole "draws the line at giving TSA officers the right to choose passengers for closer inspection based on their age, ethnicity, religion or sex. In other words, to profile."

Profiling has both tricky constitutional and practical dimensions.

Constitutional Dimensions

On the former, the operative constitutional text is the Fourth Amendment, which opens with these stirring words: "The right of the people to be secure in their persons, houses, papers, and effects, against unreasonable searches and seizures, shall not be violated. . . ."

The amendment speaks with a forked tongue. On the one hand, it is clear that the right of all people to be "secure in their persons" looks as though it is "violated" by either pat downs or body scanners. On the other hand, the use of the law's most indispensable weasel word, "unreasonable," suggests that only some searches are "unreasonable," leaving it to the fine art of constitutional interpretation to decide which ones those are.

The first gambit in favor of the government is that all searches done with consent of the individuals searched should be regarded as "per se reasonable," and thus beyond constitutional challenge. That alluring argument, however, is wrong. It is not enough that individuals who don't want to be searched are free to go back from where they came. That "take it or leave it" notion works fine in competitive markets, but not when the government operates a state monopoly, as it does with security. It is not as though United Airlines may let you board a flight without a search, even though American Airlines demands it.

That pesky word "unreasonable" has worked its way into our constitutional heritage through the text of the Fourth Amendment. We are thus duty-bound to make sense of it by asking what kinds of searches the government can properly undertake. Here we are light-years away from the invidious distinction that searches are unrelated to any legitimate government objective. It is futile for anyone to insist that it is illegitimate for the government to block efforts to blow up planes.

Racial and Ethnic Profiling

Some searches, then, are here to stay. The question is which. On this point, racial and ethnic profiling raises the most contentious issues because they involve discriminating on grounds over which no individual has any measure of control. Presumptively, we do (and should) think that these maneuvers are bad.

That observation does not end the debate, however. It only pushes the inquiry back a step. Is there any way to overcome the presumption that profiling is bad? In dealing with the issue of profiling, the question is this: If there were forms of profiling that reduced costs and increased safety, is there anything in the Fourth Amendment that makes this unreasonable?

The answer to that abstract question has to be in the negative. The very notion of reasonableness asks us to put different "reasons" on both sides of the moral balance beam. Reducing costs is always a good thing, as is increased safety. To attack this position is to insist that it is only reasonable for one to pay more in the form of dragnet searches in order to get less in the form of protection against criminal attacks.

So ultimately, the question is do we get more by concentrating on particular groups? In answering that question, Pistole made reference to the Israelis who for years have made aggressive use of racial profiling in order to keep down the obvious risks of a terrorist attack. While some might insist that this is "arguably" unconstitutional, ultimately, even a small government libertarian like myself has to conclude that it is manifestly constitutional. Much as one has to be uneasy about any exercise of government discretion, sound discretion is what it takes to run any complex government service. There is no way to wish discretion away in the operation of legitimate government agencies.

Practical Concerns

The question, then, is whether comparing the U.S. to Israel here makes sense. Pistole insists that it does not. Rather than put words in his mouth, let me quote what the *Wall Street Journal* has to say:

> Mr. Pistole says that can't be replicated here. Israel is a small country with 50 daily flights; America has 456 airports and 27,000 flights. "It's not as straightforward as in Israel where

they have a lot of experience with how to separate" suspects, he adds, saying that terrorists here don't necessarily fit a profile. Examples include dirty bomber José Padilla and Oklahoma City bomber Tim McVeigh.

These arguments just do not hold water. Sure Israel has fewer flights in and out. We have thousands more. But Israelis also devote fewer resources to their task than we do. The issue isn't the difference in the size of the endeavor, it is how best to run the system with the available resources. Perhaps we cannot and should not use profiling at all locations, but we could surely start with the 50 most dangerous flights and work up from there. Start with New York, and move on to Modesto later.

As to experience, the only way to acquire it is through intensive catch-up efforts right now. Hiring a few Israelis as consultants might help speed the process along. Surely the Israelis know that some suspects will not fit the standard profile. Indeed we can go one step further. In this game of cat and mouse, we can be sure that any determined terrorist organization will do the unexpected by adopting fiendish counterstrategies to evade our first line of defense.

It is, however, just a non sequitur to say that we should abandon profiling just because terrorists have counterstrategies. If we can implement our first-best strategy, we can force terrorists to adopt their second-best strategy, which already lowers the odds of a catastrophic loss. It is not always easy for even a determined adversary to switch the point of attack.

Think of it this way. If a Muslim group from Yemen, say, wants to recruit a blond-haired Westerner to commit suicide, the group runs all sorts of risks. Finding a Westerner who believes in the culture of willing death for a higher cause is hard, meaning the terrorists run the risk of hiring someone who will fink out or turn over valuable evidence to the United States. Indeed, we can capitalize on that uncertainty by dispatching government agents who could lure the terrorist groups into a trap that will allow us to gain valuable access to terrorist networks.

How to Profile at American Airports

The hard question is to figure out how to profile. And one key element is to be sensitive of the needs of those individuals who are members of the targeted races and nationalities. Managing racial sensitivities is unpleasant business, as are body scans and pat downs.

In a world in which everyone concedes that absolute security is not attainable, it is unwise, even dangerous, to unilaterally renounce a technique that has yielded positive returns elsewhere. Our skies have been safe for nearly the past ten years. We have to take all prudent steps, even unpleasant prudent steps, to make sure that this streak of good fortune continues.

> "And it is here, at the grounded cross-roads of aviation and commerce, that civil liberties and public safety collide with government power ostensibly designed for our mutual protection."

Profiling Is Not an Effective Security Strategy

Sam Fulwood III

Sam Fulwood III is a senior fellow at the Center for American Progress. In the following viewpoint, he points out that recent calls for racial and ethnic profiling as a security strategy are misguided. Fulwood contends that not all terrorists neatly fit into certain racial and ethnic categories; in fact, he notes, there have been a number of American-born terrorists who have pulled off horrible attacks—and they would not have raised flags in a security system based on racial and ethnic profiling. He argues that the inconvenience and indignity of modern airport security strategies must be endured by all passengers who choose to fly.

As you read, consider the following questions:

1. Who is John Tyner, according to the author?

2. What conservative columnist does Fulwood identify as supporting racial and ethnic profiling?

3. What homegrown terrorists does Fulwood name as examples of those who wouldn't fit in easy profiling categories?

I travel a great deal on commercial airliners but I can't remember the last time I noticed the signs at the airport warning against cracking jokes about hidden bombs in suitcases or weapons in fanny packs. Surely those bulletins are still prominently displayed at the security gates and ticket counters but I'm probably overlooking them because of the clutter of warnings about the Transportation Security Administration's [TSA's] new and intrusive physical screening policies at the nation's airports.

Controversial Screening Policies

Federal officials say the best way for them to ferret out hidden bombs on a traveler's person is to get intimate with them at the boarding gates. Since 2007, some airports have installed full-body scanners which make X-ray-like images of the folds and contours of the human body. But that's not the worst of it. In some cases, when the images show something suspicious, TSA officials may use open palms to touch genitalia and other private body areas.

News reports of these new security measures brought angry reactions from some air travelers. Notably airline pilots objected, saying the security measures were unnecessary for them. Others complained the procedures went too far, lumping people deemed unlikely to be terrorists—the elderly, women with children, airline pilots, and flight crews—among those who really might be, as if anyone could really tell the difference among the multiethnic variety of terrorists willing to target innocent civilians.

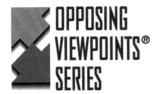
OPPOSING
VIEWPOINTS®
SERIES

make us afraid, and make our government do exactly what the TSA is doing. When we react out of fear, the terrorists succeed even when their plots fail. But if we carry on as before, the terrorists fail—even when their plots succeed.

Periodical and Internet Sources Bibliography

The following articles have been selected to supplement the diverse views presented in this chapter.

Joel Dreyfuss	"On Airport Security, Do We Really Want to Be Like Israel?," *PostPartisan* (blog), *Washington Post*, November 24, 2010.
Nathan Guttman	"Israel's Airport Security, Object of Envy, Is Hard to Emulate Here," *Jewish Daily Forward*, January 6, 2010.
Froma Harrop	"Why Profiling Can't Ensure Airline Security," Creators.com, January 11, 2010.
Farhana Khera	"New Travel Directive Is Wrongheaded," *Progressive*, January 8, 2010.
Charles Krauthammer	"Don't Touch My Junk," *Washington Post*, November 19, 2010.
Heather MacDonald	"Sensibly Selective Screening," *National Review Online*, January 6, 2010.
Eugene Robinson	"Why Granny Gets Searched," *Washington Post*, November 23, 2010.
Noah Shachtman	"Is Common Sense Coming to Airport Security?," *Wall Street Journal*, August 10, 2011.
Bret Stephens	"Our Incompetent Civilization," *Wall Street Journal*, January 4, 2010.
USA Today	"Our View on Airport Screening: Why Israel's Air Security Model Wouldn't Work in the USA," December 21, 2010.

CHAPTER 4

What Ongoing Issues Affect Airport Security?

Chapter Preface

One of the most notorious tools the Transportation Security Administration (TSA) uses to protect the US airline industry from terrorist attacks is the No Fly List. Maintained by the Terrorist Screening Center (TSC), a division of the Federal Bureau of Investigation (FBI), the No Fly List is made up of the names of people prohibited from boarding a commercial airliner for flight in or out of the United States because of suspected terrorist activities or terrorist ties. As of February 2012, the list had twenty-one thousand names of known or suspected terrorists on it. About five hundred of those on the list are Americans.

The No Fly List has generated much controversy in recent years. One reason is that the government does not have to explain to an individual why his or her name is put on the list, making it harder for a person to defend himself or herself. There have been numerous instances of travelers being mistaken for people on the list, an occurrence known as a false positive; for example, if a person has the same name as a suspected terrorist, he or she can be detained for hours at the airport until the confusion has been cleared up. If a traveler knows that he or she has been put on the list erroneously, it is difficult to get his or her name removed. As a result, many innocent travelers have been stranded in foreign airports and seriously inconvenienced because of mistakes, false positives, or bureaucratic ineptitude.

US government officials argue that the list is essential to protecting the US airline industry from another terrorist attack like that on September 11, 2001. They also point out that recent improvements to how the list is compiled and maintained have made it even more effective in fighting terrorism and protecting the civil liberties of individuals. For example, it is constantly under review by authorities to make sure that names put on it in error are removed and that new threats are noted.

The history of the No Fly List can be traced to the years before 2001, when the Federal Aviation Administration (FAA) issued a series of occasional security bulletins to commercial airline companies. After terrorists successfully brought down Pan Am Flight 103 over Lockerbie, Scotland, on December 21, 1988, the FAA was tasked with advising airlines of security risks and intelligence information that would be useful to them. Sometimes the security directives included the names of people the intelligence community deemed serious threats to the industry. On September 10, 2001, there were about twenty names on the FAA's list of potential threats.

The terrorist attacks of September 11, 2001, prompted a government committee to review the intelligence and security failures that led to the attacks. The members of the committee were outraged that although the US State Department had identified sixty-one thousand people as suspected or known terrorists, the FAA had warned the airline industry about so few. It was clear that improvements had to be made to better protect the nation's aviation industry from a repeat of the September 2001 attacks.

The No Fly List quickly expanded. By December 2002, it included around one thousand names. By 2006 it was reported that the list had more than forty-four thousand names on it. Maintaining the list was a responsibility transferred from the FAA to the TSC. There was more cooperation between intelligence agencies to identify potential and existing threats. In addition to the names of individuals known to have planned terrorist attacks against airliners or airports, the list grew to include suspected terrorists, family members, and known associates. In fact, the exact criteria for adding names to the No Fly List are a closely guarded secret.

Despite reports of improvements, there are still numerous stories of innocent travelers detained and searched at airports because their names appeared on the No Fly List. For many, it remains a key part of an overall security strategy to safeguard the US aviation industry. For critics, it is a tool used by an ever-growing government to harass and limit the travel of Americans and foreign visitors—especially young Muslim men. In recent years, there has been a growing call to abolish the No Fly List altogether.

The debate over the No Fly List is just one of the issues examined in the following chapter, which covers ongoing controversies in airport security. Other viewpoints explore the implications of collective bargaining on the TSA, privatizing airport screening, improving the selection and training of TSA screeners, and abolishing the TSA.

"The point is that good solutions are more likely to emerge regularly and consistently under a robust market dynamic than under government monopoly."

Privatizing Airport Screening Would Improve Security and Efficiency

Nick Schulz and Arnold Kling

Nick Schulz and Arnold Kling are the authors of From Poverty to Prosperity: Intangible Assets, Hidden Liabilities and the Lasting Triumph over Scarcity. *In the following viewpoint, they suggest that one way to improve the security of US airports is to privatize airport security. In such a scenario, the private sector would be responsible for the design and implementation of airport security. Schulz and Kling argue that a market-based system would reward private companies able to adapt to emerging threats; satisfy customers by facilitating speedy and efficient passenger screening processes; and continually reassess and improve procedures, training, and technology to remain competitive.*

As you read, consider the following questions:

1. According to the authors, why was the TSA created by Congress?

2. What two government functions do the authors envision in a market-based airport security system?

3. What does the Defense Advanced Research Projects Agency do, according to the viewpoint?

After the underwear bomber's attempted mass murder [on a plane en route to Detroit on December 25, 2009], Americans are losing patience with the airline security system. It is bad enough that our screening process makes innocent people work far too hard to prove that they are not terrorists. It also manages to make it too easy for actual terrorists to be treated as innocent.

President [Barack] Obama said the security system failed "in a potentially disastrous way." He's right. So how can we improve it?

The security process needs several things it is lacking. It needs continuous adaptation, with a strong focus on satisfying customers and improving results. It needs to find new and better methods of meeting the demands of customers who value safety as well as speed and efficiency. It needs to function in a dynamic environment, disciplined by rigorous competitive pressure.

In short, it needs the market.

Keeping the Focus: Safety

Let's stipulate at the outset that many details would need to be worked out and could be determined only after a market concept is embraced. That said, here's how it could work and why it would be an improvement over the status quo.

Responsibility for the design and implementation of airline security should be handed back to the private sector. But make no mistake: This system would look nothing like the pre–9/11 [referring to the terrorist attacks on the United States on September 11, 2001] private system that treated terrorism like the distant threat we believed it was. The Transportation Security Administration (TSA) was created by Congress, after all, for one reason: The previous system failed catastrophically. But the attacks didn't succeed because it was a private system. The attacks succeeded because—quite simply—we lived in a pre–9/11 world, one in which knives and box cutters could be carried aboard U.S. airplanes.

A post–9/11 market system would combine the benefits of a competitive system with the much stricter federal oversight necessary to ensure a basic standard of travel security. Airlines would select firms to screen passengers who will fly on their planes. Let's say that it would be up to each airline to contract with at least one security firm at each airport. The airline would pay the firm a set dollar amount per passenger, and this cost would be passed along through ticket prices.

Of course, security firms that offer low cost to airlines and low hassle to passengers would, all else equal, be able to win more business from airlines already looking to cut expenses. But if security companies are competing to keep costs and hassles to a minimum, what would keep security itself from becoming too lax?

Incentive Mechanisms

Several incentive mechanisms, some of them market based, would keep private sector firms focusing on safety. First of all, the flying public may show a preference for airlines that employ security firms with rigorous procedures—just as today many drivers prefer safer cars that get lower gas mileage.

Second, if a private firm were to allow a single failure or even a near miss, it would immediately lose the confidence of fliers. Airlines would switch to other suppliers, and the flawed firm would go out of business.

Security companies also could be required to be liable for damages up to, say, $25 million from terrorism, and to post bond to cover that liability. (It is harder to sue the government for damages than the private sector.)

The government's role would include two functions. It would collect intelligence on high-risk suspects (as it does today) and share this intelligence with private airline security firms—which will require the firms to have robust data security. And the government would audit private security companies, with the power to impose fines if lapses are found. The government could still ensure, for instance, that every firm at least meet the minimum standards that the TSA employs today.

The audits would cover data security (government intelligence information used by the firms and personal privacy must be protected); the design of processes for segmenting passengers according to risk; the design of screening procedures that are appropriate for each level of risk; and the implementation of those screening procedures.

The policies and procedures would no doubt vary for different security companies. But this is a feature, not a bug, because only through differentiation and innovation can new techniques emerge to meet evolving demands of safety and efficiency. For example, one firm might rely heavily on passenger interviews, as the Israeli airline El Al is known for. Another firm might rely more on the latest scanning technology. Companies might vary their rules for boarding and carry-on luggage by passenger risk category—low-risk passengers could take their liquids and gels and keep their shoes on, while high-risk passengers would have to check such items or scan them.

Improvement via Competition

We do not know what sorts of policies and procedures would emerge. The point is that good solutions are more likely to

Rethinking Airport Security

It is time to reevaluate the assumption made in the 2001 Aviation [and] Transportation Security Act, or ATSA, that aviation security is an inherently governmental function. The private sector with appropriate government oversight is fully capable of handling the security responsibility currently performed by government transportation security officers. In fact, a recent Government Accountability Office study found that when considering both "cost and performance" there is little to no difference between the government and private sector.

P.J. Crowley and Lindsey Ross,
"How to Make the TSA (and Airports) Work Better," Center for
American Progress, April 2, 2009. www.americanprogress.org.

emerge regularly and consistently under a robust market dynamic than under government monopoly. Competition will force even the lowest quality provider to raise standards year after year by adopting the good ideas that emerge from their competitors. This is why even a cheap automobile today has more amenities than a luxury car of 30 years ago.

What's more, our national security establishment is increasingly seeing the benefits of competition. DARPA [Defense Advanced Research Projects Agency], the agency responsible for developing some of the military's cutting-edge technologies, has instituted its Urban Challenge [also known as the DARPA Grand Challenge], which offers cash prizes to the private sector competitors who fight it out to solve technology problems. The notion of using market dynamics to meet pressing national security needs is not academic.

While most passengers don't realize this, the TSA itself permits a handful of airports, such as Kansas City and Rochester, to use private security contractors under its Screening Partnership Program. But much more should be done to unleash a genuinely competitive market so that the benefits of competition—in terms of improved service and technological innovation—can be realized more swiftly.

No security system will be perfectly safe, of course, including a market-based system. And many changes would no doubt need to be considered, including to airport infrastructure. But the advantage of a market system over a "one-best-way" government monopoly is that the incentives to innovate and find new solutions for safety as well as convenience are sharpened and refined by steady competitive pressures.

> *"It became clear to many of us that aviation security was inseparable from national security, and we could not, and should not, rely on the private sector to do the job."*

Privatizing Airport Screening Would Threaten Security

Joe Lieberman

Joe Lieberman is a US senator from Connecticut. In the following viewpoint, he opposes the idea that the responsibility for airport security should revert back to private contractors instead of the Transportation Security Administration (TSA). Lieberman reminds House and Senate members of how private security failed passengers on September 11, 2001, when terrorists were able to board planes with objects that were used as dangerous weapons. He argues that aviation security is inseparable from national security, and the American government cannot rely on the private sector to do the job. Therefore, any attempts to undermine the ability of the TSA to work effectively is misguided and ill-advised in his opinion.

Joe Lieberman, Statement Regarding the Federal Aviation Administration Modernization and Reform Act, US Senate Committee, February 7, 2012.

As you read, consider the following questions:

1. According to Senator Lieberman, how many short-term funding extensions did the Federal Aviation Administration (FAA) need in a four-year period?

2. How does Lieberman describe the Screening Partnership Program (SPP)?

3. How many senators were part of the bipartisan group that introduced the legislation that would create the TSA, according to the viewpoint?

M r. President. I rise today [February 7, 2012] to voice my support to the Federal Aviation Administration Modernization and Reform Act conference report which was passed by the Senate last night, and will provide a greater sense of financial security than the Federal Aviation Administration (FAA) has seen in a long time. No agency should be subjected to the budget uncertainties that FAA has been forced to experience, nor strung along year after year unable to make long-term plans. For more than four years, the FAA has operated under more than 20 short-term funding extensions. I think that is unprecedented in the history of agency funding. At any rate, it is no way to run a railroad, or a national aviation system.

I also support the conference report because it would finally allow the FAA to move forward on the NextGen [Next Generation] air navigation program; would give the Passenger "Bill of Rights" the force of law; and would provide billions of dollars to improve and develop public airports across the country. For these reasons, the legislation is long overdue and sorely needed.

The conference report, however, does contain a provision about aviation security and the Transportation Security Administration (TSA) that is deeply troubling to me and about which I feel duty-bound to express my disapproval.

The Screening Partnership Program

At stake is TSA's management of the Screening Partnership Program (SPP), which allows a limited number of airports around the country to replace transportation security officers (TSO) with private contractors to screen passengers and their baggage. TSA has implemented this program at airports where, due to low traffic volume, full-time, year-round federal staff is unnecessary. A handful of larger airports take part in the program so TSA can measure and assess its performance and cost effectiveness against the private contractors. It is telling that TSA's assessment after comparing the two systems is that it can secure airports more economically than private screeners can.

Regrettably, some of my colleagues in the House and Senate are resolved to undermine TSA—and therefore airport security itself—by advocating for the pre–9/11 [before the terrorist attacks on the United States on September 11, 2001] system of screening by private contractors. My response to that is: How quickly we forget. Mr. President, we have already tried an aviation security system run by private contractors. It very tragically did not work. The 9/11 attacks did not occur because of one, two, or three specific vulnerabilities. They occurred because a number of our defenses—including our system of airport screening—were simply inadequate.

I know everyone has vivid memories of the days after the 9/11 attacks, and it is hard to forget the dramatic loss of confidence the public felt for the aviation security system. Air travel dropped off precipitously in the weeks and months after 9/11, the aviation industry was shaken to its core, and our economy suffered because of it.

A Government Responsibility

It became clear to many of us that aviation security was inseparable from national security, and we could not, and should not, rely on the private sector to do the job. The security of our skies would have to become a government responsibility. Americans need to be safe and secure wherever and whenever they traveled. And while I would not want to cast blame or criticism on any one contractor, we've already witnessed the results of a system utilizing private security companies which were constantly pressured to focus on costs first, and security second.

Less than two weeks after the 9/11 attacks, a bipartisan group of 21 senators introduced the legislation that would create TSA and turn airport screening over to federal officials. Barely a month after 9/11, the Senate passed that bill by a vote of one hundred to zero. The bipartisanship of that vote was heartening and demonstrated a unity among members that I wish we could experience more often. In the years since, we have had a few near misses, and our defenses have been penetrated more than once, but no hijackings or terrorist incidents have been successfully carried out. In large part, we have a dedicated corps of TSOs to thank for that.

Necessary Policies

I know it is fashionable in some quarters to criticize TSA. Understandably, people are unhappy with pat downs, body scans, and invasions of privacy. But TSA establishes its policies for a reason. They are a direct response to real terrorist threats. And they have evolved as the threat has evolved. When a terrorist put explosives in his shoes and tried to light them afire midflight in 2001, TSA asked passengers to remove their shoes for screening. When a terrorist plot was uncovered in 2006 that involved lighting flammable liquids aboard several planes, liquids, except in small quantities, were prohibited. After the Christmas Day 2009 attempted attack with explosives hidden in a terrorist's clothing, better screening technology was developed. These are not hypothetical cases or academic scenarios. They are real incidents and the reason that TSA makes so many demands on the flying public. And we should not delude ourselves or the American people into thinking that adopting a contract workforce will eliminate the need for body scanners, pat downs or any other security procedure TSA determines is necessary to secure air travel; regardless of whether a U.S. airport uses federal screeners or private ones, the security procedures implemented are the same.

A Core Mission

Yet, a provision has been tucked into this bill that would make it more difficult for TSA to maintain its current system by lowering the burden of proof for admitting additional airports to the Screening Partnership Program. Right now, airports must demonstrate that a private screening workforce would be more effective, secure, and efficient, than the TSA. The standard tucked into this bill, however, "would only require airports to demonstrate that using private screeners would not compromise security or detrimentally affect the cost efficiency or the effectiveness of screening."

While the TSA administrator would still have the authority to deny an application to the Screening Partnership Program, this lower standard would make it far more difficult for him to do so. TSA administrator [John S.] Pistole has said that the Screening Partnership Program should be used judiciously and that airport screening is and should remain a core mission for the Department of Homeland Security since 9/11, and I agree with him wholeheartedly.

Another provision in the bill strikes me as counterproductive. This provision would require TSA to provide recommendations to an airport that was denied its application to the SPP on how that airport can overcome the denial, if it decides to resubmit its application. If TSA believes that it can screen passengers and baggage better and with more cost efficiency than a private contractor, why would it provide tips on how an airport can escape that system?

Strengthening Airport Security

Private screening could also limit TSA's ability to react nimbly to intelligence threats. If screeners are privately employed and managed airport by airport, TSA may not be able to respond effectively by shifting personnel to where it is most needed or modifying procedures if it cannot exert direct control over screeners.

Mr. President, private screening at airports could undermine not just public confidence in the aviation security system but in aviation security itself. We have been there and experienced the consequences of private screening. The American public must feel secure when it travels, and security is the first priority of TSA.

Ultimately, I voted for the Federal Aviation Administration Modernization and Reform Act. But I believe we should reconsider and revisit the language related to TSA's Screening Partnership Program. I would urge my colleagues to remember the lessons learned after 9/11 and work with me to ensure we won't make the same mistakes again.

> *"Security guards with minimal training cannot be expected to exercise discretion in critical matters.... The result is that screaming children are being felt up by strangers and the sick and elderly are publicly humiliated."*

Airport Screener Selection and Training Must Be Improved to Ensure National Security

William John Cox

William John Cox is an author and political activist. In the following viewpoint, he asserts that improving the existing Transportation Security Administration (TSA) personnel selection system is necessary to effectively and efficiently protect airport security. Cox states that the current employment process at the TSA "perpetuates mediocrity" because it fails to rank applicants by qualifications or suitability for the positions offered; this gives managers little to no discretion in hiring and allows unqualified applicants to obtain jobs. He suggests that the TSA reassess its employment and training procedures and focus more on arming transportation security officers with greater discretion to implement a risk-based security strategy at US airports.

As you read, consider the following questions:

1. According to Cox, how many websites have something to say when you Google "TSA stupidity"?

2. What does Cox say are the basic requirements for TSA officers?

3. How many millions of people does Cox say travel by air annually?

Google "TSA stupidity" and you will find that almost one-and-a-half million websites have something to say about the subject. If the United States is to avoid another major terrorist attack on its air transportation system without placing greater restrictions on the civil liberties of air travelers, the Transportation Security Administration (TSA) had better get smart.

Everyone who travels by air in the United States has a depressing story to tell about airport screening. Media stories of a gravely ill 95-year-old grandmother forced to remove her adult diaper before being allowed on a plane and viral videos showing terrified children being intimately touched by TSA agents are more than depressing. They are a chilling commentary on the police state increasingly accepted by the American public in the name of security.

Air travelers dare not complain. TSA standards focus additional scrutiny on travelers who are "very arrogant" and express "contempt against airport passenger procedures."

Is such repression the only choice? Or, can TSA officers be trained to exercise the necessary discretion to detect would-be terrorists while allowing innocent travelers to swiftly and safely pass through screening?

A reasonable and practical balance in airport security screening policy must be obtained before another terrorist attack results in even greater repression.

Today's TSA

Shocked that poorly trained airport security guards allowed terrorists armed with box cutters to board and use four passenger airplanes as flying missiles of mass destruction, Congress established the TSA two months after 9/11 [referring to the terrorist attacks on the United States on September 11, 2001].

Fifty thousand transportation security officers (TSO) were quickly hired and rushed through one-week training courses. Although these officers are now federal employees and receive improved training, they are still security guards. Even so, as "officers" of Homeland Security, they exercise great power over the flying public.

TSA transformed contract screening guards into quasi–law enforcement officers and provided uniform training and policies; however, the TSA was organized as a top-down directed organization which allows very little discretion to individual officers. It's "one-size-fits-all" approach to screening results in well-intended, but outrageous, conduct by its agents.

In an attempt to prevent collective bargaining and to avoid adding Democratic-leaning permanent workers to the federal bureaucracy, the Republican-controlled Congress exempted TSA employees from most federal civil service laws. Instead, the secretary of Homeland Security and the TSA administrator were given virtually unlimited authority to create a personnel system. This action was to have a number of unintended consequences.

Although legislation has been introduced to bring TSA officers into the federal civil service, the TSA administrator retains absolute control over the personnel system. Exercising this power, administrator John [S.] Pistole granted some bargaining rights earlier this year [in 2011].

The TSA Personnel Selection System

While Pistole's order provides greater job protection to officers, it does nothing to improve the existing TSA personnel selection system. As presently constituted, the employment process perpetuates mediocrity and limits the ability of TSA managers to hire and promote the most qualified officers.

Currently TSA job applicants primarily use the Internet to identify job announcements for TSA airport operations at more than 450 airports, complete applications and take an online test to measure their ability to operate screening equipment.

All English-speaking U.S. citizens over the age of 18 with a high school diploma, a GED [general equivalency diploma], or one year of experience as a security officer or X-ray technician, meet the basic requirements for TSA officers, as long as they are current in their payment of income taxes and child support.

The main problem is that, once applicants meet these minimum requirements and pass a physical examination, drug screening and perfunctory background investigation, they are lumped together with all other applicants in a hiring pool for each job site.

Unlike general civil service rules, there are no ranked lists of the most qualified applicants within these pools.

Under the personnel standards established by the TSA administrator, local managers are required to select officers from the hiring pool based on the earliest applicant first, irrespective of their additional qualifications. Thus, a local TSA manager must hire a high school dropout with a GED and no experience who applied one day before a college graduate with a degree in criminal justice and who earned his or her way through college working for the campus police department. While some managers conduct oral interviews of candidates, only in rare cases are they allowed to reject candidates who meet the minimum qualifications.

Mission Effectiveness

Laboring under a flawed selection process and making the best of available candidates, TSA has identified three basic ways to achieve mission effectiveness: baggage inspection, passenger screening and, most recently, behavior observation.

Although every checked bag is not hand inspected, passengers are not allowed to lock baggage unless special TSA locks are used. As a result, most bags are inspected by inspectors who are either working alone or under limited supervision.

There have been some recent improvements in baggage security; however, the *New York Press* reports that "according to Transportation Security Administration records, press reports and court documents, . . . approximately 500 TSA officers" have been "fired or suspended for stealing from passenger luggage since the agency's creation. . . ."

Every passenger is personally screened before boarding commercial aircraft and the majority of TSA officers are deployed to handle this task. Having a mission in which officers "literally touch passengers" and their most private possessions "requires a workforce of the best and brightest" according to Nico Melendez, TSA public affairs manager of the pacific region.

Unfortunately, because of low hiring standards and minimum training, many, if not most, screening officers possess poor people skills and manage to offend a large portion of the flying public on a daily basis.

Behavior Detection Officers

Seeking to emulate the Israeli model of "identifying the bomber, rather than the bomb," TSA deployed behavior detection officers (BDOs) in 2007 under its Screening of Passengers by Observation Techniques (SPOT) program. Officers randomly ask passengers questions, such as "Where are you traveling," while looking for facial cues that might indicate deception or terrorist intent, leading to additional questioning and closer inspection of baggage.

Thousands of BDOs are now working in hundreds of airports and the program is being expanded; however, they are generally selected from screening personnel and only given two weeks of training before being deployed.

There has been no scientific validation of the program and, although there have been hundreds of criminal arrests, most have been for documentation issues, such as immigration violations and outstanding warrants.

Would improved personnel selection procedures of TSA officers better ensure the safety of the flying public and reduce the incidence of civil rights violations?

Building a Better TSA

The essential question is whether TSA officers are security guards or police officers when it comes to the manner in which they lay hands on the bodies and belongings of passengers. The difference in the two roles being the manner and extent to which they make decisions.

Security guards with minimal training cannot be expected to exercise discretion in critical matters. They are told exactly what or what not to do. The result is that screaming children are being felt up by strangers and the sick and elderly are publicly humiliated.

On the other hand, even with the "mandatory" criminal laws passed in the past 30 years, America's free society still requires the exercise of arrest, prosecution and sentencing discretion in the criminal justice system, if there is to be individual justice in an individual case.

TSA must rethink the manner in which its officers are hired and trained to allow greater discretion, without an unacceptable rise in the risk of a terrorist attack.

The TSA has been moving in this direction with its "risk-based, intelligence-driven screening process"; however, its steps have been hesitant and unsure, as it has staggered from incident to increasingly negative incident.

Melendez believes the key to successful screening is a workforce capable of implementing a risk-based screening process based upon updated software and equipment and ready access to an improved database.

So, how can a marginally trained group of 50,000 security guards be converted into a professional workforce, which has the intellectual ability and training to use sophisticated detection equipment and computer databases and which allows TSA officers to decide which sick person or young child should be allowed to proceed without a mandatory body search?

Selection Should Be Based on Qualifications

A former high-level TSA manager, who declined to be publicly identified, firmly believes that TSA could build an elite organization, if local managers were simply allowed to rank the hiring pools by qualifications, rather than having to hire the candidate who filed the earliest application.

Certainly there is a need to avoid discrimination in hiring and to create a "diverse and inclusive" workforce that is reflective of the public it serves; however, police departments have used a civil service process for decades that involves testing and interviews to establish priority lists to ensure the employment and promotion of the most qualified candidates.

Among the federal law enforcement agencies, the FBI [Federal Bureau of Investigation] moves applicants through a multiphase selection process in which advancement depends upon "their competitiveness among other candidates"; Secret Service applicants must pass several examinations and a series of in-depth interviews; and ATF [Bureau of Alcohol, Tobacco, Firearms and Explosives] applicants who pass entrance exams and assessment tests have to successfully complete a "field panel interview."

A Prime Opportunity

The current recession and high unemployment rate have resulted in a gigantic pool of highly qualified and well-educated people who are looking for work. At the same time, TSA has been experiencing a fairly high turnover of employees, even though it offers a generous salary and benefits package. Given all of this, there is a golden opportunity to improve the quality of the TSA workforce, particularly as it relates to the ability of its officers to exercise discretion.

A recent informal survey of airport car rental employees revealed that all of them were college graduates; however, they generally earned less and had fewer benefits than the TSA officers who worked in the same building.

In fact, most national car rental companies require all applicants to have college degrees. Avis says, "College graduates, start your engines" in its attempt to attract "energetic proactive college graduates who are eager to accelerate their careers in a fast-paced environment." Enterprise "prefers" college degrees since applicants will "be involved in a comprehensive business skills training program that will help you make crucial business decisions. . . ."

Clearly it is neither necessary nor appropriate for all TSA applicants to be college graduates; however, local TSA managers should be allowed to consider levels of education, as well as length and quality of relevant experience, in establishing priority lists for hiring replacement officers and for promoting officers to supervisory or BDO positions.

Revised personnel policies that rank applicants by qualifications for these advanced positions would also allow TSA managers to directly hire more qualified candidates, such as retired police officers, for positions requiring a higher level of decision making.

Training Must Be Done in Classrooms

Currently, most training of TSA officers is conducted through online applications of standardized instruction. While such training may be adequate to communicate rule-based procedures to security guards, it is inadequate to teach the more finely nuanced insights required for officers to safely exercise discretion in individual cases.

Behavior detection officers and supervisors are currently selected from the ranks of TSOs and receive as little as two weeks of additional training upon promotion. However, a successful risk-based screening process involving critical thinking requires more intensive development and training.

Obviously, TSA can't fire 50,000 officers and start all over again from scratch, but surely there is a way to safely maintain the basic security guard approach to screening yet allow for higher levels of discretion during the process.

Assuming that TSA managers are allowed to more effectively promote officers and to select supervisors and behavior detection officers from outside the organization, and further that TSA could improve the training of supervisors and BDOs, they could begin to exercise the quality of discretion which would allow small children and elderly grandmothers to safely pass through security without impermissible assaults.

TSA should consider establishing regional training academies at the larger facilities around the country to provide classroom training for newly appointed supervisors and BDOs into the nature of policy, the concept of rational profiling and the exercise of security discretion in a free society.

Policies Must Have Clear Guidelines

The concept of policy, as differentiated from procedures and rules, is that policies are intended as broad guidelines for the exercise of discretion allowing decision makers some flexibility in their application.

The exercise of critical discretion will fail in the absence of effective policies. This was recognized by the National Advisory Commission on Criminal Justice Standards and Goals in its report on the police in 1973:

"If police agencies fail to establish policy guidelines, officers are forced to establish their own policy based on their understanding of the law and perception of the police role. Errors in judgment may be an inherent risk in the exercise of discretion, but such errors can be minimized by definitive policies that clearly establish limits of discretion."

We are all aware of the insidious and repressive nature of racial profiling that has been practiced by some law enforcement agencies. Indeed, one criticism of the TSA behavior detection program that involved Newark BDOs known as "Mexican hunters" was that they concentrated on Hispanic-appearing individuals, resulting in a large number of arrests for immigration violations.

Finding the Right Focus

Well-considered policies can allow BDOs to productively direct their attention to the most suspicious candidates for extended questioning, rather than to mindlessly and repetitively ask every single traveler where they are going.

With improved policy guidance and greater discretion, BDOs might actually identify and stop a real threat, but they will only offend even more travelers if they continue to follow rote procedures.

Perhaps most importantly, such polices can provide commonsense guidelines for qualified decision makers at each screening station to allow obviously harmless grandmothers and children to avoid intrusive body contact while focusing attention on those individuals more likely to be a terrorist.

The Right Direction

According to TSA 101, a 2009 overview of the TSA, the agency seeks to evolve itself "from a top-down, follow-the-SOP [standard operating procedure] culture to a networked, critically thinking, initiative-taking, proactive team environment."

TSA administrator John [S.] Pistole wants "to focus our limited resources on higher-risk passengers while speeding and enhancing the passenger experience at the airport."

On June 2, 2011, Pistole testified before Congress that "we must ensure that each new step we take strengthens security. Since the vast majority of the 628 million annual air travelers present little to no risk of committing an act of terrorism, we should focus on those who present the greatest risk, thereby improving security and the travel experience for everyone else."

It appears TSA is moving in the right direction and John Pistole may be the person to keep in on course. Prior to his appointment by President [Barack] Obama in May 2010, he served as the deputy director of the FBI and was directly involved in the formation of terrorism policies.

Most significantly, his regard for civil rights was suggested by his approval of FBI policy placing limits on the interrogation of captives taken during the "war on terror." The policy prohibited agents from sitting in on coercive interrogations conducted by third parties, including the CIA [Central Intelligence Agency], and required agents to immediately report any violations.

Hopefully, Mr. Pistole will exercise his authority to bring about improved selection and training of TSA personnel and will promulgate thoughtful screening policies, which will result in a safer and less stressful flying experience for everyone.

"*[The Transportation Security Adminis-
tration] must be abolished totally and
nothing short of that will bring liberty
back to air travel.*"

The Transportation Security Administration Is Incompetent and Should Be Disbanded

Anthony Gregory

*Anthony Gregory is a research editor at the Independent Insti-
tute. In the following viewpoint, he maintains that the Transportation Security Administration (TSA) is inefficient, incompetent,
and violates the privacy of individuals. Gregory characterizes the
TSA as an agency that was not designed to protect airline passengers but as a government tool used to condition obedience
and enforce subservience to federal power. The only way to re-
gain freedom, he argues, is to completely abolish the TSA and let
airports find ways to protect passengers from terrorism. Gregory
also notes that as long as the US government continues to fight
wars overseas and meddle in the policies of other countries, there
will be a potent threat of terrorism in the United States.*

Anthony Gregory, "TSA Abuses: Seeing the Forests and the Trees," Future of Freedom
Foundation, June 30, 2011. Copyright © 2011 by The Future of Freedom Foundation.
All rights reserved. Reproduced by permission.

As you read, consider the following questions:

1. What was the heritage of Richard Reid, according to Gregory?

2. According to a December 2010 report, what was the failure rate of airport screeners at some major airports in the United States?

3. According to the author, who is Rigoberto Alpizar?

The Transportation Security Administration [TSA] is finally getting some of the bad publicity it deserves. We read about an elderly woman forced to remove her adult diaper to go through the screening process. We learn about a mentally disabled passenger deprived of his harmless toy by a sadistic policy, if not sadistic TSA agents. We see pictures of women and little children being felt up, all the while Americans stand by, seemingly helpless to do anything about such humiliations. A whole country has been conditioned to these summary body scans and pat downs, these invasions of bodily integrity that would have unlikely been tolerated in the era before 9/11 [referring to the terrorist attacks on the United States on September 11, 2001], a memory that grows dimmer by the day.

The Conservative Reaction

Under [President Barack] Obama, conservatives once again pose as advocates of liberty, increasingly expressing outrage about TSA abuses. They are right to be angry. We could ask where they were almost ten years ago when their president, George W. Bush, oversaw the creation of this national monstrosity. More to the point, we should note that their critique hardly goes far enough and is somewhat misdirected.

The conservatives complain that grandmas and helpless children are being abused, and instead the TSA should pursue a more "common sense" policy that streamlines unthreatening people through a less invasive process. Those who obviously don't "look like a terrorist" shouldn't be molested. Sounds good. But what many of them mean is that we need racial profiling, and that Arabs, Muslims, and those from questionable nations should undergo extra scrutiny. Yet this too is objectionable and absurd. Hundreds of thousands if not millions of such people fly in America regularly, and only an infinitesimal fraction are any threat. Why should the government subject innocent Arabs and Muslims to indignities and unreasonable searches without due process? On the other hand, British citizen Richard Reid, the attempted "shoe bomber" of December 2001, didn't look like a "typical" terrorist. He was of European and Jamaican descent. TSA agents are simply not equipped to discern who is a threat from who is not, and they never will be. There is no way to guarantee the total security conservatives have spent a decade demanding while preserving the liberty of everyday Americans.

The Liberal Reaction

The liberals are even more disgraceful. They spoke up for civil liberties under Bush, decrying the No Fly List and other such depredations. Now many of them, suspicious of the conservative TSA critics, defend this terrible agency created by Bush and made worse under Obama. They even cheer as TSA agents vote to unionize, as though better compensating these federal employees or making them even harder to fire should be on the top-ten-thousand list of priorities for any humanitarian, as the Left claims to be. Even worse, many Left-liberals have denied that these screening procedures are intolerably invasive. Some have said those on the No Fly List should be barred from gun ownership. The same liberals who fret about big business's threats to the environment and consumer safety defend the TSA full-body scanner, insisting the health risks are a total fantasy.

Security Fail

In March [2011], *USA Today* reported that the TSA "would retest every full-body X-ray scanner that emits ionizing radiation—247 machines at 38 airports—after maintenance records on some of the devices showed radiation levels 10 times higher than expected." The same government that many Americans trust to protect their health didn't even bother to accurately test within an order of magnitude the radiation levels of its equipment before irradiating many millions of Americans and foreigners. And why should anyone be subjected to this risk, no matter how small? Ah yes, for the privilege to fly.

Some will say that this is simply the price we pay for security, but that is a complete illusion. According to ABC reporting last December, TSA diagnostics to determine how many weapons could be snuck past security found that some major airports had a failure rate of 70% and at some airports, "every test gun, bomb part or knife got past screeners." Nothing has improved since college student Nathaniel Heatwole snuck weapons onto a plane at Baltimore-Washington International [Thurgood Marshall] Airport back in September 2003 and then e-mailed his story to the TSA, which took five weeks to find the contraband. A flustered top TSA official insisted, "Amateur testing of our [security] systems do not show us in any way our flaws. We know where the vulnerabilities are and we are testing them." Eight years later, have they addressed these vulnerabilities? A determined terrorist, needless to say, could easily infiltrate a plane with weapons.

No wonder that when terrorists are stopped in their tracks—the shoe bomber of 2001 and the underwear bomber of 2009, for example—they were frustrated by the private sector, flight crew and customers, and not by TSA. This has happened without major casualties inflicted on the innocent—unlike the case of Rigoberto Alpizar who in December 2005 was shot multiple times on a Miami runway by two air marshals, who claimed the man had cried out he had a bomb, something none of the passengers corroborated. Moreover, when people actually stop a terrorist incident, it has nothing to do with mass invasions of the personal privacy of millions of airline customers.

Disband the Transportation Security Administration

In nearly a decade, there is not a single report of a terrorist having been caught during the TSA [Transportation Security Administration] screening process. No bombs have been discovered. No hijackings have been thwarted. For the TSA to claim it has made the nation's skies safer is as absurd as the rooster taking credit for the sun rising each morning. Observant passengers have caught more terrorist wannabes than the 67,000 TSA employees.

Mark Hyman,
"Disband the TSA," American Spectator,
November 23, 2010.

The Answer Is Private Security

Airlines have every reason to protect their property and their customers, which means private security—not as it was before 9/11, overseen by the FAA [Federal Aviation Administration], but truly, completely private security—is the answer. (The recent resignation of the major FAA official due to the scandalous tendency of his air traffic controllers to be caught sleeping on the job indicates just how indispensible and crucial *that* agency is.)

In a free market for security, some airlines might have detailed screening processes. Others might allow guns on planes—another defensive approach that has been completely neglected. Whether airlines profile or not will be up to them, but customers will demand security without violations of their dignity, and the private sector, unlike government, has all the incentives to deliver on both fronts.

The myopic focus on planes is questionable to begin with. What about other, similarly vulnerable, public locations? Will they come to mirror the authoritarian atmosphere of the airports? The TSA has already terrorized Amtrak passengers and has its eyes set on other ground transportation—is this really the direction we want this country to go? Recently the agency was even involved at securing a high school prom.

Abolish the TSA

The missing fact in most of the controversy is that TSA is neither truly designed nor institutionally structured to protect us. We are not really surrendering our gels, forgoing our bottled water, or taking off our shoes for our own good. That's all a ruse. The TSA is an agency whose function, if not intended purpose, is to condition obedience and subservience into the population. It is an arm of the federal police state and cannot be reformed into anything else. It must be abolished totally and nothing short of that will bring liberty back to air travel.

Even more fundamentally, the media and talking heads—certainly the conservative opponents of TSA—forget why we have a terrorist threat, such as it is, in the first place: Because the U.S. government is waging imperial wars abroad, slaughtering children, propping up corrupt regimes, overthrowing governments, playing geopolitical favorites, cutting people off of international trade, and generally behaving as the biggest bully in the world. The blowback terrorism that results can never be stamped out so long as the wars continue. Those who criticize the TSA but defend the wars, and those who defend the TSA but question the wars, should recognize they are two sides of the same imperial coin. The same statism behind the degradation of domestic passengers is in play in the dehumanization of foreign civilians bombed from the sky. Washington, D.C., sees itself as master of our lives and ruler of the world. So long as we accept its pretensions to control the planet, we will be treated as imperial subjects are always treated: as mere cogs in the machine, disposable and malleable human livestock, at the very best.

| *"The No Fly List is a punishment in search of a crime."*

The No Fly List Does Not Enhance Security and Should Be Abolished

Steve Chapman

Steve Chapman is a columnist for the Chicago Tribune. *In the following viewpoint, he recommends eliminating the No Fly List, which contains the names of hundreds of US residents who are considered too dangerous to be allowed to fly. Chapman points out that Americans have the constitutional right to travel freely, as is recognized by the US Supreme Court. He believes that if the people on the list are truly dangerous, they should be arrested and tried in a court of law. If not, let them travel without restrictions. He also argues that there have been several important improvements to airport security in the last few years that the rationale behind the list is no longer valid.*

As you read, consider the following questions:

1. What organization does Chapman give credit to for suing on behalf of travelers who were wrongly put on the No Fly List?

Steve Chapman, "A Radical Proposal for Airline Security," *Reason*, July 19, 2010. By permission of Steve Chapman and Creators Syndicate Inc.

2. According to Chapman, in what year did the US government mandate that all travelers show government-approved identification before boarding a flight?

3. What particular flight does Chapman mention as an example of passengers acting to foil attacks?

If a job not worth doing is going to be done anyway, better for it to be done well than badly. So the Transportation Security Administration [TSA] deserves credit for its Secure Flight program, aimed at curbing mistakes on its No Fly List. The American Civil Liberties Union, likewise, warrants praise for suing on behalf of travelers who were wrongly snared.

Get Rid of the List

But there is a better option that would eliminate this problem, as well as others: Get rid of the No Fly List entirely. For that matter, get rid of the requirement that passengers provide government-approved identification just to go from one place to another.

Americans have a constitutionally protected right, recognized by the Supreme Court, to travel freely. They also have the right not to be subject to unreasonable searches and other government intrusions. But in the blind pursuit of safety, we have swallowed restrictions on travel and infringements on privacy we would never tolerate elsewhere.

The No Fly List is a punishment in search of a crime. As Richard Sobel, a director of the Cyber Privacy Project and a scholar at Northwestern University, points out, it inflicts a penalty without a trial or any other form of due process.

The TSA doesn't say what it takes to get on the list, and it doesn't make it crystal clear how to get off. If it acts in an arbitrary or malicious way, the victim has little recourse except appealing to the agency's better angels.

No Rationale for the List

But the whole idea behind the list doesn't make much sense. Supposedly, we have hundreds or even thousands of U.S. residents who are too dangerous to be allowed on a plane—but safe enough to be trusted in all sorts of other places (subway trains, sports venues, shopping malls, skyscrapers) where someone carrying a bomb or a gun could wreak havoc.

If those on the list are truly dangerous, the government should arrest and prosecute them, with their guilt decided by courts. If they are not dangerous enough to arrest, they should have the same freedom to travel as everyone else.

We don't prohibit all ex-convicts from flying. How can we justify barring people convicted of nothing?

But there is a broader problem. If the federal government began requiring every citizen to provide identification for each trip in a car or ride on a bus, there would be a mass uprising. Somehow, though, Americans have come to see commercial air travel as a privilege to be dispensed by the government.

It was not always so. Not so many years ago, Sobel notes, you could show up without a reservation or a ticket at Washington's National Airport (now Reagan National Airport), walk onto the hourly shuttle to LaGuardia [Airport in New York], take a seat and pay your fare in cash. No one knew who you were, and no one cared.

A Change in Policy

But in 1995, Washington mandated that all travelers show government-approved identification before boarding a flight. The freedom to travel without federal permission was gone. The No Fly List further limited that liberty.

After 9/11 [referring to the terrorist attacks on the United States on September 11, 2001], the requirement served the purpose of helping keep violent fanatics off airliners. What no one seems to notice is that other improvements in security have made this one a needless burden.

The List Continues to Grow

The [President Barack] Obama administration has more than doubled, to about 21,000 names, its secret list of suspected terrorists who are banned from flying to or within the United States, including about 500 Americans. . . .

The size of the government's secret no-fly list has jumped from about 10,000 in the past year, according to government figures provided to the AP [Associated Press].

Eileen Sullivan,
"No-Fly List of Suspected Terrorists More
than Doubled in Past Year," Huff Post Travel,
February 2, 2012. www.huffingtonpost.com.

The government required airlines to install reinforced cockpit doors to keep hijackers from taking the controls. It tightened security rules—banning penknives, lighters, ski poles, snow globes, and liquids except in tiny bottles.

It initiated random pat downs of travelers and gave extra scrutiny to those who did suspicious things. It deployed thousands of armed air marshals.

A Defensive Mind-Set

Equally important, travelers changed their mind-set, meaning that terrorists can no longer count on passive victims. On several occasions—starting with United [Airlines] Flight 93 on 9/11—passengers have acted to foil attacks.

With all these layers of protection in place, the rationale for the No Fly List has crumbled. Even if someone on the list can get on a plane, his chance of taking it over or bringing it down is very close to zero. And you know the other good thing? The same holds for an aspiring terrorist who doesn't make the list.

The government's tedious insistence on identifying all travelers and grounding some may convey an illusion of security. But we could live—and I do mean live—without it.

> *"Forcing the Transportation Security Administration to collectively bargain with its airport security screeners' union would endanger Americans."*

Allowing Airport Screeners to Collectively Bargain Would Weaken Security

James Sherk

James Sherk is a fellow in labor policy in the Center for Data Analysis at the Heritage Foundation. In the following viewpoint, he argues that facilitating collective bargaining rights for the employees of the Transportation Security Administration (TSA) will endanger Americans. Sherk maintains that the TSA cannot be caught up in fraught negotiations when it needs to be flexible in light of rapidly changing security threats. Also, he asserts that keeping a merit pay system will keep employees motivated and promote the best officers in the most sensitive positions. He also points out that airport screeners have a voice when it comes to working conditions and improving security practices and strategy.

As you read, consider the following questions:

1. According to Sherk, how many security screeners have joined the American Federation of Government Employees (AFGE)?

2. How long did it take the TSA to overhaul its security procedures after attempted British airline bombings in 2010, according to the author?

3. What does Sherk say was the TSA's voluntary attrition rate in 2006?

Members of Congress have tucked into the Implementing [Recommendations of] the 9/11 Commission Act of 2007 (H.R. 1) and the Improving America's Security Act of 2007 (S. 4) a provision to weaken America's national security that the commission never recommended. The bills would require the Transportation Security Administration (TSA) to collectively bargain with government unions representing airport security screeners. Collectively negotiating every change in work procedures or duty assignments would significantly reduce the ability of the TSA to flexibly respond to terrorist threats and other emergencies. Moreover, TSA screeners already have a voice, are able to join unions, and leave their jobs less than private sector transportation workers. This provision has no place in legislation intended to make Americans safer.

Collective Bargaining Is at Issue, Not Union Membership

When Congress created the TSA, it gave the agency the authority to decide whether or not to engage in collective bargaining with airport baggage screeners. The TSA concluded that collective negotiations would impair its ability to protect the American people, and the 9/11 Commission [formally known as the National Commission on Terrorist Attacks Upon the United States] never suggested otherwise. Nonetheless, members of Congress have inserted a provision requiring the TSA to collectively bargain with airport screeners into the legislation intended to implement the commission's recommendations.

At issue is whether or not the TSA must collectively bargain with government unions before it changes personnel and policies, not whether TSA employees should be allowed to join a union. Much of the news coverage has gotten this wrong. Airport screeners may voluntarily join a union today, and the TSA will withhold union dues at an employee's request. Seven hundred security screeners have chosen to become dues-paying members of the American Federation of Government Employees (AFGE). The union, however, has no standing to collectively bargain with the TSA. The new provision would require collective negotiation of personnel assignments and promotion policies.

Less Flexibility to Respond to Threats

The TSA needs the maximum flexibility to respond to potential threats using the latest information available. It needs the ability to rush screeners to high-risk locations and modify screening procedures at a moment's notice. It has this flexibility now. Following the attempted U.K. [United Kingdom] airline bombings last summer [2010], for example, the TSA overhauled its procedures in less than 12 hours to prevent terrorists from smuggling liquid explosives onto any U.S. flights.

The TSA cannot spend weeks or months collectively negotiating new procedures or personnel assignments before implementing them. Collective bargaining would impose such delays. Other government unions in the Department of Homeland Security have strongly resisted changing established procedures and the flexible assignment of personnel. The National Treasury Employees Union (NTEU), for example, brought the Customs and Border Protection (CBP) before an arbitrator after the CBP unilaterally changed policies without collectively negotiating first. The arbitrator found that the CBP should have provided the NTEU with notice and the opportunity to bargain before the CBP made its changes, such as the Port of Houston reassigning officers to the [George] Bush [Intercontinental] Airport and the Port of New Orleans implementing a new master schedule.

The TSA does not have weeks to bargain over officer assignments and new schedules before implementing them. It needs the flexibility to act immediately to protect Americans. Collective bargaining introduces a layer of bureaucracy and delay that America cannot afford.

Merit Promotions Protect National Security

Today airport screeners earn their promotions through merit and competence, not seniority. The TSA evaluates screeners on the basis of their technical proficiency, training and development, customer service skills, teamwork, professionalism, and leadership, and then awards promotions, raises, and bonuses to high performers. This allows the TSA to assign the best screeners to the most sensitive posts and to keep screeners motivated despite the potential tedium of their jobs.

Most government departments place considerable weight on seniority when promoting employees because government unions insist on it in collective bargaining. If Congress gives unions the chance, they are all but certain to insist on seniority-based promotions at the TSA. The AFGE has already sued the TSA for laying off workers who performed poorly on tests of skill without taking into account their seniority. Seniority-based promotion systems may make life easier for many workers, but they would harm national security. America needs the best and most motivated screeners in the most sensitive positions, not those who have simply been on the job the longest.

Screeners' Voices Are Heard Today

Airport screeners do not need collective bargaining because their voices are already heard. Screeners can already join a union, and the AFGE represents its members in grievance procedures and job safety complaints. The TSA has created a career progression initiative to create a career track for screeners without resorting to seniority-based promotions. The TSA has also created employee advisory councils to address workplace issues and designed its merit pay system with consultation and feedback from 4,000 employees.

Reflecting their job satisfaction, screeners are less likely to leave their jobs than private sector workers in comparable positions. The TSA's voluntary attrition rate was 16.5 percent in 2006, while in the private transportation–utilities sector, 19.6 percent of workers left their jobs that year. Airport screeners have a voice and are heard by management at every level and, so, do not need collective bargaining.

Forcing the Transportation Security Administration to collectively bargain with its airport security screeners' union would endanger Americans. The TSA needs the flexibility to rapidly move officers and overhaul procedures without first spending weeks in collective negotiations. Merit pay systems, which unions resist, keep screeners motivated and ensure that the best officers serve in the most sensitive positions. Even without collective bargaining, the TSA listens to airport screeners and takes their advice when changing work conditions. Congress should remember that the TSA exists to protect American lives, not guarantee workers a stable work schedule or seniority-based promotions. Its mission requires flexibility that collective bargaining would foreclose.

Periodical and Internet Sources Bibliography

The following articles have been selected to supplement the diverse views presented in this chapter.

Becky Akers	"Abolish the TSA, and Let the Markets Protect Passengers," Forbes.com, May 26, 2011.
Mike Elk	"Union: Media's Portrayal of TSA Employees Has Hurt Our Bargaining Power," *In These Times*, January 2, 2012.
Ed Feulner	"TSA and Big Labor: A Bad Union," *Indianapolis Star*, February 24, 2011.
Douglas French	"TSA Unionization May Open Floodgates," *Christian Science Monitor*, March 2, 2011.
Conor Friedersdorf	"Ron Paul Seeks to Abolish TSA, Despite Its 500 Cute Puppies," *Atlantic*, July 6, 2011.
Carol Platt Liebau	"The Obama Administration's TSA Giveaway," Townhall.com, February 7, 2011.
Jena Baker McNeill	"TSA Privatization Freeze: More Politics than Security," Heritage Foundation, February 2, 2011. www.heritage.org.
Bruno J. Navarro	"Is It Time to Abolish the TSA?," CNBC.com, May 3, 2012.
John Nichols	"A Great Big Win for Labor and (Real) National Security: 40,000 TSA Screeners Go Union," *Nation*, June 23, 2011.
Kimberley A. Strassel	"Ready for Unionized Airport Security?," *Wall Street Journal*, March 11, 2011.
Robert VerBruggen	"Unionizing the TSA," *National Review Online*, February 11, 2011.
Washington Times	"Union Power at TSA," February 8, 2011.

For Further Discussion

Chapter 1

1. After reading all six viewpoints in the chapter, what is your overall opinion on airport security? Do you believe that Americans are safer on airlines since the terrorist attacks on the United States on September 11, 2001? Explain your reasoning.

2. In his viewpoint, Patrick Smith argues that airport security has the wrong focus. Do you agree or disagree? What should be the priority when it comes to airport security?

Chapter 2

1. Recent changes in passenger screening policies have been extremely controversial. Is the new approach more effective in protecting commercial air travel? Read all seven viewpoints in the chapter to inform your answer.

2. Rand Paul contends that invasive security policies undermine security and violate civil liberties. Robin Kane and Lee Kair disagree. Which argument do you believe is more persuasive, and why?

3. In his viewpoint, Josh Nathan-Kazis maintains that passenger screening procedures may violate religious modesty. How important is privacy when it comes to security matters? Is it okay to violate religious modesty in the interest of protecting airports and passengers? Explain your answer.

Chapter 3

1. Richard A. Epstein recommends profiling as a security strategy. Sam Fulwood III argues that profiling is not a security strategy. Which author makes a stronger argument, and why?

2. Should the United States adopt the Israeli approach to airport security? Why or why not? Read viewpoints by Stephanie Gutmann and Pierre Atlas to inform your answer.

Chapter 4

1. There has been a growing movement to privatize airport screening. Do you believe that this would improve security or threaten it? Read viewpoints by Joe Lieberman and Nick Schulz and Arnold Kling to inform your answer.

2. Read all six viewpoints in this chapter and identify the one suggestion you feel could significantly improve airport security. Explain your reasoning.

Organizations to Contact

The editors have compiled the following list of organizations concerned with the issues debated in this book. The descriptions are derived from materials provided by the organizations. All have publications or information available for interested readers. The list was compiled on the date of publication of the present volume; the information provided here may change. Be aware that many organizations take several weeks or longer to respond to inquiries, so allow as much time as possible.

Air Line Pilots Association, International (ALPA)
1625 Massachusetts Avenue NW, Washington, DC   20036
(703) 689-2270
website: www.alpa.org

The Air Line Pilots Association, International (ALPA) is the largest international pilot union, representing more than fifty thousand American and Canadian pilots. Established in 1931, ALPA advocates for the interests of airline pilots with the airline industry, government officials, business leaders, and federal agencies. Another central aspect of its mission is to lobby for safety and security improvements in the airline industry. ALPA national and local safety and security committees are made up of more than six hundred airline pilots who are knowledgeable about current practices and intent on improving safety and security for passengers and staff. The ALPA website offers information on breaking news; position papers on topics of interest; statements and testimony from top officials at ALPA; and access to *Air Line Pilot Magazine*, a monthly periodical that gives in-depth coverage of the industry.

Airline Pilots Security Alliance (APSA)
One Park Lane, Suite 412, Boston, MA   02210
(615) 479-4140
e-mail: apsa@secure-skies.org
website: http://secure-skies.org

The Airline Pilots Security Alliance (APSA) is a nonprofit organization made up of volunteers from the airline industry who offer "expert information and guidance to the public and policy makers to implement sensible and effective aviation security measures." APSA works closely with law enforcement, pilots' associations, the Transportation Security Administration, and the Department of Homeland Security to craft forward-thinking policies to protect the airline industry, passengers, and crew. The APSA website links to testimony, press releases, and public statements from the organization's leaders as well as to its e-mail newsletter.

Airlines for America (A4A)
1301 Pennsylvania Avenue NW, Suite 1100
Washington, DC   20004
(202) 626-4000
e-mail: a4a@airlines.org
website: www.airlines.org

The principle trade organization of the airline industry, Airlines for America (A4A) advocates for effective safety, security, customer service, and environmentally responsible policies. A4A works to foster the economic growth of the airline industry in the United States and evaluates and supports sensible government regulations and security measures. It provides a wide range of services to its members, including committees focused on airline security and safety improvements. The A4A website offers access to recent press releases, statements, testimony from experts, speeches from A4A officials, letters, position papers, court filings, and an online bookstore featuring a number of various publications.

Central Intelligence Agency (CIA)
Office of Public Affairs, Washington, DC   20505
(703) 482-0623 • (703) 482-1739
website: www.cia.gov

Established in 1947, the Central Intelligence Agency (CIA) is the civilian intelligence agency of the US government. It is responsible for gathering intelligence on foreign governments and terrorist organizations and provides national security assessments to US policy makers. The CIA's intelligence-gathering activities include assessing emerging and existing threats to the US government, monitoring and analyzing correspondence and Internet communications, implementing tactical operations in foreign countries, developing and managing intelligence assets, launching counterterrorism efforts, and dealing with threats to US computer systems. A major role of the CIA is to find information on terrorist threats to the United States, including ones to the nation's airports and airline industry. The CIA website offers a featured story archive, recent press releases and statements, speeches and testimony by CIA officials, and a page for kids to learn about CIA initiatives.

Federal Aviation Administration (FAA)

800 Independence Avenue SW, Washington, DC   20591
1-866-835-5322
website: www.faa.gov

The Federal Aviation Administration (FAA) is the US federal agency tasked with overseeing and regulating the nation's aviation industry. As an agency of the US Department of Transportation, the FAA regulates commercial airline transportation; develops and operates the air traffic control system; creates and enforces flight inspection standards; facilitates new aerospace technology and safety regulations; and investigates airplane crashes, accidents, and other aviation incidents. Another of the FAA's responsibilities is to conduct research on the nation's commercial and general aviation safety record, which can be found on the FAA website. The FAA also provides access to airport compliance records, air traffic information and guidelines, recent testimony from FAA officials, fact sheets and statistics, training resources and manuals, and regulatory information.

International Air Transport Association (IATA)

800 Place Victoria, PO Box 113, Montreal   H4Z 1M1
   Canada

+1 514 874 0202 • fax: +1 514 874 9632
website: www.iata.org

The International Air Transport Association (IATA) is an international trade group of airline companies that strives to effectively represent, lead, and serve the airline industry. The security of airline passengers is central to IATA's mission. One of its key responsibilities is the scheduling process, which determines the fair allocation of slots for airline companies at airports worldwide. IATA also publishes standards for the entire industry; launches new technology and initiatives that aim to save travelers and crew time and money; regulates the shipping of dangerous goods; and certifies the operational management of airlines through the IATA Operational Safety Audit (IOSA). IATA provides access to a wealth of information on the group and its activities, including a calendar of events, recent press releases, information on IATA training and certification programs, webinars, fact sheets, and transcripts of speeches from IATA officials.

National Counterterrorism Center (NCTC)
Office of the Director of National Intelligence
National Counterterrorism Center, Washington, DC   20511
(703) 733-8600
website: www.nctc.gov

An agency of the Office of the Director of National Intelligence (DNI), the National Counterterrorism Center (NCTC) analyzes emerging and existing threats to the safety of the United States, disseminates relevant intelligence with other government agencies and partners, develops operational strategies, and marshals the resources of the national government to address those threats effectively. NCTC also advises the DNI on intelligence analysis and operations relating to counterterrorism and serves as the central resource for all information on counterterrorism activities and intelligence. The NCTC website offers press releases, interviews, speeches and testimony from NCTC officials, published reports, fact sheets, and the legislation that established the center. There is also an

NCTC page for young children that provides an introduction to the organization and its activities.

Terrorist Screening Center (TSC)
FBI Headquarters, 935 Pennsylvania Avenue NW
Washington, DC   20535
(202) 324-3000
website: www.fbi.gov/about-us/nsb/tsc

Part of the Federal Bureau of Investigation (FBI), the Terrorist Screening Center (TSC) is responsible for maintaining the US Terrorist Watchlist, which is a single, consolidated database of all known or suspected terrorists or people suspected of terrorist activity. It also oversees the No Fly List, a much smaller list, which contains the names of people not allowed to board a commercial airliner for travel in the United States and prohibits them from flying into the country. The goal of the TSC is to effectively consolidate and maintain both the Terrorist Watchlist and the No Fly List and "facilitate the sharing of terrorism information that protects the nation and our foreign partners while safeguarding civil liberties." The TSC website features video, recent news, a blog, podcasts, stories, speeches and testimony of FBI and TSC officials, and FBI radio.

Transportation Security Administration (TSA)
TSA HQ, TSA 2, 601 S. Twelfth Street, Arlington, VA   20598
(877) TSA-7993 • fax: (877) TSA-7993
e-mail: TSA-ContactCenter@dhs.gov
website: www.tsa.gov

The Transportation Security Administration (TSA) was established after the terrorist attacks of September 11, 2001, to protect the transportation systems of the United States. It is responsible for security at the nation's airports, managing a federal workforce trained to effectively screen all passengers, cargo, and baggage. The TSA has implemented new technologies to improve the level of security for passengers and crew, including advanced imaging technology, biometric identification, bottled liquid scanners, and explosive detection system

(EDS) machines. It also works closely with international partners to share information on threats to the aviation industry in the United States and abroad, as well as coordinates and conducts security assessments at foreign airports and repair stations. The TSA website provides access to breaking news, press releases, speeches and testimony from TSA officials, fact sheets, and information on new initiatives the TSA will be implementing in US airports.

US Department of Homeland Security (DHS)
245 Murray Lane SW, Washington, DC   20528-0075
(202) 282-8000
website: www.dhs.gov

The Department of Homeland Security (DHS) is tasked with protecting the United States from terrorist attacks and other threats. Established after the terrorist attacks of September 11, 2001, the DHS aims to reduce the vulnerability of US infrastructure and installations, government officials, and major events to attacks of any kind; to enforce and administer immigration laws to better control who is traveling in and out of the country; to coordinate and administer the national response to terrorist attacks and be a key player in recovery and rebuilding efforts; and to safeguard and secure cyberspace by assessing cyber threats and coordinating a counterattack. The DHS works closely with other government agencies and relevant partners to protect the nation's airports and prevent terrorist attacks on US airliners, passengers, and crew. The DHS website allows access to a number of informative resources, including fact sheets, breaking news, press releases, videos, speeches and testimony of DHS officials, and other publications on topics of interest.

US Department of State
2201 C Street NW, Washington, DC   20520
(202) 647-4000
website: www.state.gov

The US Department of State is the federal agency responsible for formulating, implementing, and assessing US foreign policy. The State Department also assists US citizens living or traveling abroad; promotes and protects US business interests all over the world; and supports the activities of other US federal agencies in foreign countries. It oversees the Bureau of Counterterrorism (CT), which is focused on developing coordinated strategies to defeat terrorists abroad and in advancing the counterterrorism objectives of the United States. The State Department website features a wealth of information on current policies, upcoming events, daily schedules of top officials, and updates from various countries. It also has videos, congressional testimony, speech transcripts, background notes, human rights reports, and strategy reviews.

Bibliography of Books

Joseba Altarescu and Taro Bai, eds. *Aviation and Passenger Security.* New York: Nova Science Publishers, 2012.

David H. Brown *Full Body Scam: The Naked View of Current Airport Security.* Bloomington, IN: AuthorHouse, 2011.

Bartholomew Elias *Airport and Aviation Security: U.S. Policy and Strategy in the Age of Global Terrorism.* Boca Raton, FL: CRC Press, 2010.

Kip Hawley and Nathan Means *Permanent Emergency: Inside the TSA and the Fight for the Future of American Security.* New York: Palgrave Macmillan, 2012.

Susan N. Herman *Taking Liberties: The War on Terror and the Erosion of American Democracy.* New York: Oxford University Press, 2011.

Barbara Hudson and Synnove Ugelvik, eds. *Justice and Security in the 21st Century: Risks, Rights and the Rule of Law.* New York: Routledge, 2012.

Natalia Ippolito *I Might as Well Be Naked: How to Survive Airport Screening with Your Clothes On.* Enka, NC: Divineisland Books, 2007.

James Lutz and Brenda Lutz *Terrorism: The Basics.* New York: Routledge, 2011.

Gus Martin	*Understanding Terrorism: Challenges, Perspectives, and Issues.* 3rd ed. Los Angeles, CA: Sage, 2010.
Harvey Molotch	*Against Security: How We Go Wrong at Airports, Subways, and Other Sites of Ambiguous Danger.* Princeton, NJ: Princeton University Press, 2012.
Lori Peek	*Behind the Backlash: Muslim Americans After 9/11.* Philadelphia, PA: Temple University, 2011.
Jeffrey C. Price and Jeffrey S. Forrest	*Practical Aviation Security: Predicting and Preventing Future Threats.* Boston, MA: Butterworth-Heinemann/Elsevier, 2009.
Dana Priest and William M. Arkin	*Top Secret America: The Rise of the New American Security State.* New York: Little, Brown and Co., 2011.
Dan Reuter and John Yoo, eds.	*Confronting Terror: 9/11 and the Future of American National Security.* New York: Encounter Books, 2011.
Mark B. Salter, ed.	*Politics at the Airport.* Minneapolis: University of Minnesota Press, 2008.
Bruce Schneier	*Schneier on Security.* Indianapolis, IN: Wiley, 2008.
Paul Seidenstat and Francis X. Splane	*Protecting Airline Passengers in the Age of Terrorism.* Santa Barbara, CA: Praeger Security International, 2009.

David K. Shipler   *The Rights of the People: How the Search for Safety Invades Our Liberties*. New York: Alfred A. Knopf, 2011.

Daniel J. Solove   *Nothing to Hide: The False Tradeoff Between Privacy and Security*. New Haven, CT: Yale University Press, 2011.

Susan B. Trento and Joseph J. Trento   *Unsafe at Any Altitude: Exposing the Illusion of Aviation Security*. Hanover, NH: Steerforth Press, 2007.

David Tucker   *Illuminating the Dark Arts of War: Terrorism, Sabotage, and Subversion in Homeland Security and the New Conflict*. London: Continuum, 2012.

George Weigel   *Faith, Reason, and the War Against Jihadism: A Call to Action*. New York: Doubleday, 2009.

Index

A

U